Parenting as Partners

"Raise kids and stay married at the same time. This little book may just be the thing to help you do that. Vicki Hoefle helps you uncover the tough stuff to get your parenting partnership back on track. This book goes way beyond date nights."
—Heather Shumaker, author of *It's OK Not to Share* and *It's OK to Go Up the Slide*

"Vicki Hoefle's deep expertise and compassion for contemporary families comes through on every page. The insights in this book will be support parents looking to improve their co-parenting and to deepen their understanding of themselves and their children."
—Devorah Heitner, PhD, author of *Screenwise: Helping Kids Thrive (and Survive) in The Digital World*

Parenting as Partners

How to Launch Your Kids Without Ejecting Your Spouse

Vicki Hoefle

bibliomotion
inc.

First published 2017
by Bibliomotion, Inc.
711 Third Avenue New York, NY 10017, USA
2 Park Square, Milton Park, Abingdon, Oxon OX14 4RN, UK

© 2017 Taylor & Francis

Bibliomotion is an imprint of the Taylor & Francis Group, an informa business

No claim to original U.S. Government works

International Standard Book Number-13: 978-1-62956-175-2 (paperback)
International Standard eBook Number-13: 978-1-315-20584-7 (ebook)

Library of Congress Cataloging-in-Publication Data
A catalog record for this title has been requested

Visit the Taylor & Francis website at
http://www.taylorandfrancis.com

Printed and b

Contents

Introduction

Drew grew up with a mom who made sure his every need was met. She made his breakfast for him, packed his lunch, did his laundry and made life as pleasant as possible so he could be free from distraction and enjoy his childhood. His father was the king of the castle who was in charge of both the discipline and the fun. Drew looked forward to the time when it would be his turn to be ruler, living with a partner that reflected his own mother's role of attentive wife and accommodating mother. Gwen, on the other hand, grew up in a single-parent home where she was required to help out, not just occasionally, but regularly. She was making her own breakfast by the time she was five years old and was involved in every aspect of family life by the time she was ten years old. It was absolutely necessary that she and her siblings do their share to support the success of the family. She developed very strong ideas about what it meant to be a contributing and valued member of the family.

Like many couples, Drew and Gwen were initially attracted to each other because of their differences, which were influenced by their unique interpretations of life based on their individual childhood experiences.

They believed these differences would help them create a balanced life together, one in which they could draw on each other's strengths and overcome their shortcomings in the safety of a loving and committed relationship. They also appreciated the character traits that were present in the other. She was hardworking, focused and capable. He was fun loving, committed and held himself to high standards. She believed he would be the father for her children that she never had. He believed she would be a replica of his mother who had made life so pleasant for him as a child and accepted her husband as the head of the household. It was years before they realized that their ideas on parenting, which were developed based on their early childhood experiences, were negatively impacting their marriage and their ability to co-parent successfully.

Their initial conversations on child-rearing were no more than a general agreement that they would both be involved in all aspects and always act as a united front. Any details about beliefs, attitudes and values went unmentioned. When their first child was born, they were consumed by the love they felt for him and were confident that they would always work together in the best interest of their child. Without further conversation, they began their parenting journey.

Fast forward five years and another child. Life is busier, responsibilities have increased, and the oldest child's personality is emerging. Without realizing it Drew and Gwen have stopped parenting as a unified team, but rather two distinct people with very different childhood experiences that are influencing the way they each respond to their children. Drew thinks Gwen is too hard on the kids and should do more for them so they can enjoy their childhood. She accuses him of babying them and turning them into spoiled brats. He thinks she is too rigid when it comes to discipline, and she thinks he is too wishy-washy and doesn't trust that he will be consistent or effective when he disciplines. Over time, the disagreements increased until Gwen and Drew were forced to confront the fact that they were pulling their family apart.

This story is specific to a family who came to me seeking parenting help for their now ten-year-old and five-year-old children. Maybe this sounds like you or someone you know. In my own coaching practice I hear more and more stories that center on the parents' inability to co-parent successfully and less about problems with the kids. Many families follow this same pattern and find themselves in a similar situation, stuck on how to break free from their perceptions and parent their children together as a cohesive unit. It seems that the kids are highlighting the real challenge in the family. The one between the parenting partners.

The Concept

When the idea to write this book first came to me, I was sitting on a bench overlooking the ocean, allowing my mind to drift around from thought to thought. I was in Fiji recouping from an emotionally difficult year and wanted nothing more than to relax in the warm sun with good friends and read a few trashy novels. But one quiet afternoon, as I let my mind wander, the entire book came to me in a flash—it's format, the content, the layout—and just like that I knew I had to write the book. I hadn't even pitched the book idea to my publishers when I wrote the first three thousand words. Those words were confirmation that it was time for a book on this topic. When I floated the idea past my business partner, Jennifer she said, "You mean, *How to launch your kids without ejecting your spouse*?" I paused for a millisecond and then shouted, "Yes! That book!"

My Experience

While the layout of the book came to me in an inspirational flash, the content for the book has been percolating for some time. As a professional parent coach and educator I have noticed an alarming increase over the last ten years and even more so in the last two years, in the number of parents who contact me to discuss a particularly pesky and mysterious challenge they are having with their kids, only to realize that the challenge is between the parents and their inability to co-parent effectively. Their child's behavior, it seems, is the least of their problems.

Even when working with clients who could clearly articulate their desire to create a parenting approach for the long haul, our conversations would naturally cross over into their struggle to parent successfully with their partner. Oftentimes they could explain where they were getting stuck: one parent wanted scheduled bedtimes, the other more flexibility to allow time with the kids; one parent wanted sit-down dinners together, the other parent wanted to feed the kids first and then have a quiet dinner with their partner, alone. The parents I worked with might not agree on everything, but they all agreed that no matter how many times they "talked it out," they could not agree on the best approach to take with the kids, and they were frustrated and tired of going around and around on the same issues. The truth is, it's impossible to talk about a strategy that might work for both parents and kids, when the parents themselves are struggling to support each other in their co-parenting roles. In order to make progress with the kids, first we have to address the fact that the parents are often acting independently of each other with a different set of goals and expectations, instead of as a parenting team. Most parents have trouble explaining why they end up fighting about the same things, but it is clear to me as I listen to exactly what is going on. With just a few questions we can quickly identify their opposing views, challenge those views in order to find a middle ground, agree that both of their views are valid and deserve to be represented, and then work on a strategy to support the change they want to make in their parenting.

The challenge for me in these situations is that I am not a couple's coach or a therapist. I am a parenting coach, and I was initially uncomfortable crossing over into the domain of couple's counseling. I suggested to my clients that they work with a specialized counselor, but most preferred to continue their work with me. After months of resistance on my part, I finally came to understand that I was in a unique position with a unique perspective that guides parents in first resolving the discord in their parenting positions, while simultaneously helping them to agree on a strategy to bring more balance and joy into their parenting, all while implementing, say, a much needed morning routine into life with the kids.

What's at Stake

As tensions rise between parents, their ability to parent effectively is compromised, and as a result, both the children's behavior and their emotional health are put at risk. Because we are a culture convinced that kids are the ones who need fixing (thankfully this trend is changing), it's reasonable that parents place the discord in the home at the feet of the kids, rather than on the state of the individuals doing the parenting. With each passing year, parents grow further and further apart, until they are either sabotaging each other openly or have entered into a quiet battle of wills, otherwise known as a power struggle. Without a course correction, not only are the children impacted in a negative way; the marriage suffers enough that parents consider divorce their only remedy for an untenable situation. What is most disheartening about this cycle is that it doesn't have to be this way. By taking just a few proactive steps, parents can arm themselves with the skills necessary to navigate through even the most tangled and emotionally charged situations with their partner. But only if parents take the time to create a cohesive plan that (1) takes into account that their childhood experiences (as well as their partner's) are influencing how each of them make their current parenting decisions and (2) allows them to create a strong partnership with agreements on how to handle specific situations based on the needs of their children, rather than on their own childhood experiences and the beliefs developed as a result of those experiences.

Things Have Changed

So, how did we get here? One could argue that there are dozens of reasons we find ourselves struggling to co-parent our kids successfully. I believe there are three primary reasons that make it difficult to co-parent successfully, and I believe the reasons intersect in a way that may explain why there hasn't been a more robust conversation about the changing dynamic of parenting. I also believe it is time to dive into this subject matter with gusto. This book is an invitation to any parent who is willing to explore their childhood experiences, and gather valuable information they can use to create a cohesive, unified, intersecting, parallel (call it what you will) parenting plan with their partner. If something doesn't change soon and if this trend continues, more and more will be published on how to co-parent *after* divorce rather than how to co-parent in order to *avoid* divorce.

Number One

Roles of Men in the Family Have Changed

Men are taking a more active role in the family, and as a result, their perspectives, their values and their family history are all part of the equation. Not long ago, parenting was primarily left to mom. Dad went along with mom's decisions unless the decision crossed over into his domain, which sometimes included discipline, finances, driving the car or employment. Somewhere along the way, when moms invited dads to be more "hands-on," they neglected to consider that it also meant that dad would get a say in things like sleeping policies and family meals, homework involvement and technology use, to name just a few areas of life with kids. Suddenly with two people in the mix (who, by the way, might have opposing ideas), life became more complicated for everyone in the family.

So here we are, another generation deeper into the co-parenting construct which includes two very involved parents, with no direction on how to create a collaborative, intersecting parenting plan to raise the children. Few of the parents I spoke with said they had given any consideration to the impact that having an equal partner in their parenting journey would have on their relationship, let alone the impact on their children.

Number Two

There Is No Model for Collaboration

Having raised five children I know firsthand how much adult conversation revolves around our kids, whether it's in the grocery store, the school playground, a soccer game, a cocktail party or a board meeting. We talk about our kids. We talk about the challenges we are facing, and we find comfort knowing that other parents are struggling with these same challenges. But if the conversation shifts over to our co-parenting lives, suddenly what we hear are crickets; "What do you mean a plan for co-parenting?"; or criticism of our partner who just doesn't seem to "get it," or is too harsh, too lenient, too rigid, too unpredictable, too something or other. I can't say that when my kids were young and I was consumed with parenting that I was ever part of a deep and honest conversation about how difficult it is to co-parent with someone who has very different ideas about child-rearing than you do. So why is it so difficult to tackle this subject?

First, it is difficult for parents to identify that the real problem is that they each might have different ideas on how to raise the kids, which is not a problem that can be solved with a parenting strategy for an easier bedtime or for dealing with a sassy preteen. As I have said, we are a culture that assigns more family struggles on the kids, and as a result, we put our focus there instead of on the adults who are responsible for making the parenting decisions.

Second, there are very few resources in the form of books, blogs, or workshops available to parents on the importance (rather, the necessity) for creating a cohesive and sustainable parenting plan that works for both individuals responsible for raising the children, or how to actually create the plan and then execute it.

Third, if conversations about co-parenting are being had, they usually include complaining about our partner to a close friend, rather than on brainstorming ideas on how to co-parent successfully with someone who has different ideas on how to raise the kids.

And finally, even when partners are made aware of the fact that their differing ideas on parenting is the problem, the idea of suddenly working together to create a cohesive and inclusive parenting plan seems rather daunting, sometimes untenable and in many cases just downright horrifying. So much time has been spent defending positions that working together seems like not so much a giant step toward each other, but rather a monumental leap of faith into the abyss.

Number Three

Different Childhood Experiences Inform Our Parenting Decisions
The most important factor in this equation is our lack of understanding when it comes to the impact our childhood memories play in our parenting decisions and our ability to work with, rather than against, our parenting partner.

It's natural that you and your partner would have different ideas on how to raise kids. You undoubtedly have different ideas about where to vacation, how to spend your leisure time, how many social invitations to accept in the course of a month, how to decorate your home, how important exercise is to a healthy life, how much to put into your retirement account, what kind of car to buy, and so on. Why do we think that a short conversation about raising another human being is all that is required of us? And why doesn't it occur to us that we are going to have to spend a significant amount of time collaborating with our spouse if we want to co-parent successfully from birth till—well, until we are unable to parent any longer because the truth is parenting doesn't stop just because we have successfully launched the kids into adulthood.

Once a couple identifies that their inability to co-parent effectively is undermining their efforts to raise emotionally healthy children, they can often put their differences aside and begin a dialogue which is supportive in nature and allows them to begin working with each other rather than against each other. As they begin to experience the initial thrill that comes from supporting and cooperating with each other, the cycle of hurt, blame, resentment, alienation and disconnection slowly starts to diminish. It's easy to understand why helping a couple parent as a team is not only good for their marriage; it's good for the kids as well.

Your Parenting Partnership

Your parenting plan is designed by both of you using your own childhood experiences as a launch pad. You will both explore the beliefs, attitudes and values you adopted from your own childhoods to help craft a living, dynamic plan for making unified decisions in the best interest of your children. Its aim is to minimize disagreements by bringing clarity, understanding and acceptance to otherwise fuzzy, gray areas where hidden beliefs can influence the decision making process and your ability to work together as a team.

If you are not yet parents, I encourage you to get to know your future partner's family history first. If you already have kids, then this plan is the best resource to help you navigate the established positions and learn about the foundation of your partner's upbringing.

Note: The contents of the book apply to any union charged with the responsibility of co-parenting. At times, for simplicity's sake, I use the he/she format. This in no way mitigates the partnerships between two mothers and or two fathers or grandmother and daughter or any other combination of parenting partners.

My hope is that this book will become a guide that you can refer to over and over again as you navigate the tricky terrain of co-parenting by exploring your own upbringing and shedding light on your beliefs, preferences, attitudes and values concerning parenthood. It will help both you and your partner as you develop strategies that allow you to work with your spouse in developing and implementing a cohesive parenting plan to support your marriage and your children from infancy to adulthood. In a nutshell, the purpose of this book is to help you launch your kids without ejecting your spouse in the process.

1

Why Now?

Some of the parents I work with are experiencing family problems that are solved by a specific tweak to their parenting repertoire. For many of the other parents, the real challenge before them is their inability to co-parent cooperatively. When I make this suggestion, they nod their heads fervently in agreement. These parents know this is a very real problem. What I know is that this isn't just happening to the parents who work with me and that they are not alone in their concern and their desire to find a solution that will bring them closer together as parenting partners and ensure their family stays intact. Nobody wants to launch their kids successfully while ejecting their partner from the equation, but that is exactly what is happening.

Take a moment and consider just how many areas there are for misunderstandings between you and your partner when it comes to raising children. You are reading this book because your list is already quite long or you have some strong ideas about how you want to raise your kids. Just imagine if your spouse/partner tried to challenge these ideas? What would you do? Unfortunately, for most couples the parenting plan is a generalized conversation early on in their dating or cohabiting life, and this is all the air time this incredibly important topic gets. In fact, it might not be more than agreeing on limited screen time, established bedtimes, observing religious holidays and the use of time-outs to handle discipline problems. We shouldn't be surprised when we run into difficulty finding the same page as our partner, let alone working from the same play book, when we haven't spent the time flushing out all the ideas we have about what it means to be a good, loving, competent parent, let alone how we actually plan to raise respectful, responsible, kind, hard-working and polite kids.

Before a couple begins to work at decoding the mystery surrounding their difficulty in co-parenting effectively with their life partner, it's important to understand how we all got here in the first place.

Let me say now that I am not a researcher, and I haven't spent ten years gathering data by way of scientific studies, but I can tell you that I have been working with parents exclusively for more than twenty-five years, and sometimes those of us in the trenches identify the trends long before the research supports it. Because of this I want to focus on what I believe are the three main reasons parenting with a partner is more difficult in today's world than it was in the past.

Invitation for Dad

Until the 1950s, it was safe to say that there was one parenting expert in the home, and it was usually mom. The other parent seemed content and in some cases resigned to play his part, which might include the *wait till your father gets home* disciplinarian dad, the *wait till daddy gets home* playtime dad or the *wait till dad gets home, I'm tired and I need a martini, so your father can decide if we are signing you up for little league or not* dad. In fact, roles were so clearly defined that other than a few minor squabbles between parents, life was predictable, and most major decisions as well as the hundreds made between breakfast and bedtime were made by mom.

Enter the eighties and nineties, when fathers were officially invited to take a more active role in the raising of the kids and were not only expected to accept the invitation but to participate enthusiastically and with 100% commitment to the job. Anyone remember the movie *Mr. Mom*, which came out in 1983? Well if you missed it, Michael Keaton was initially mortified and overwhelmed at the job of being a mother, but he soon learned what all primary caregivers know. When it comes to kids, the benefits outweigh the hardships.

In 2008 when the *New York Times* entered the world of parenting blogs, they titled their entry "Motherlode" and were questioning this title even then as accurately representing the parenting landscape. Eight years later they updated their blog title from "Motherlode" to "Well Family" to include the snapshot of today's modern family. Now in 2016 parenting is not limited to mom and dad, but includes combinations of two mothers, two fathers, grandparents and numerous other combinations of those charged with raising kids.

My experience working with families suggests that the intention behind the invitation is often where the seed of misunderstanding and conflict began. Inviting fathers to help out meant different things to different moms. One mother explained, "I didn't want the responsibility of a messed up kid to land squarely in my lap because I played the expert. I wanted my partner's input on every aspect of our child's life so we could share the successes and the failures." For another mother, the invitation meant "an extra pair of eyes, ears and hands so we don't leave a child or diaper bag behind, added energy and emotional support when I am running on empty and from time to time, I'd love to hear some of his ideas on where we should keep the backpacks." And for others, it was with trepidation and a bit of regret that they agreed to share the child-rearing responsibilities with their partner, because "they felt like they couldn't do anything without being criticized."

Herein lies the problem. Without clear expectations of what was included in the invitation, confusion erupted and with it a landscape readymade for disagreements, disappointment and discord.

Surprising or not, dads seemed to jump at the chance to become more involved in the raising of their kids. One could argue that they weren't entirely sure what they were getting into, but I think most dads had a sense that they were missing out on some pretty yummy stuff by allowing mom to take the lead. Dad may have interpreted the invitation to mean he would be an equal partner in the raising of the kids, which included sharing not just his brawn but his brains along with his opinions, ideas and preferences and wholeheartedly believed they would be given serious consideration.

Imagine his surprise when suggestions on how best to rock a fussy infant into slumber, or how to wash the hair of a toddler in the tub, or what snack to pack for the picky preschooler were either ignored or vetoed without even the slightest consideration. And what about his ideas on bedtime, dinnertime and playtime, not to mention discipline techniques, sibling rivalry, homework habits and technology time? Were they to be discounted as irrelevant and ignored as well? One can imagine how quickly dad might swallow his ideas, solutions and thoughts after being dismissed with some regularity. By the time the kids hit the end of elementary school, it is no surprise to find Dad back on the sidelines, where there is more listening than sharing.

What a shame to have lost our partner's ideas and perspectives when ultimately we could benefit and celebrate the fact that we have someone who is as interested and committed to the raising of our children as we are—someone who is willing to go out on a limb and share a new perspective that could benefit the entire family.

For mothers, inviting dads to be full partners meant that in spite of the fact that they were the ones who invested countless hours reading the books, scouring through blogs, listening to advice from everyone she knew and sifting through all that information to find the best plan for raising the kids, she would have to share the decision making with her partner. One mother confided, "I was a walking encyclopedia and I was willing to teach my partner the 'proper' way to feed, burp, change, play, hold, etc., based on what I learned, but he wasn't all that receptive. He kept saying, 'I'm sure there are hundreds of ways to hold, feed and burp a baby,' and each time he said it, I would blow steam out of my ears. All that research for nothing." For some it was having an over eager partner who was open and willing to be "trained" but wanted to understand the reasoning behind each of her decisions. "He couldn't just do it. He had to know why we were doing it this way or that way. I just started ignoring him, which infuriated him, and truthfully, I think I really hurt his feelings by shutting him out."

Exasperated and confused that they couldn't seem to work together without conflict arising, parents turned their attention to their children. They searched out a parenting coach, a class or workshop, a book or a blog post, to help them solve the "kid" problem, and believed that once that was handled, everything else would work out as well. But here is where my experience comes into play: no matter how sound the strategy is to deal with the children, it rarely works if both parents still hold the same beliefs that they started with, that got them into this predicament in the first place. And oftentimes, their ideas are in direct conflict with each other.

In many of my parenting classes, I remark that it is our best thinking that got us here, and if that's the case, then it's time to challenge our thinking, and in this case it means helping a couple learn what it will take to come together as a unified team whose primary goal is to raise their children in an atmosphere of respect, cooperation, collaboration and support.

A Collaborative Journey

When I first started to notice the subtle shift in my coaching conversations, I went looking for resources that would help parents learn why it was important to collaborate with their partner and how to create a cohesive parenting plan if they wanted to maintain a healthy marriage and parenting partnership for the long haul. You can find any number of books, classes, workshops and support groups on the subject of co-parenting after divorce, but almost nothing on why it is

important to create a cohesive parenting plan with your partner or how to create one, as a way to not only avoid divorce but
enjoy the lifelong journey of co-parenting kids from infancy to
adulthood. Also available to couples are thousands of articles
on how to keep your marriage alive while you are in the
trenches with kids, but again, these resources offered maintaining date night and being a united front rather than on how to
co-parent when you each have different ideas on what is best
for the kids. I was stunned at how little information is available
for parents on the subject.

Jon and Jess met in college, and although they came from
very different backgrounds there was an immediate connection and attraction. Jon was stable and reliable, and Jess was
spontaneous and unpredictable. When they talked about parenting, they imagined a perfect blend of their personalities,
idiosyncrasies and styles. They identified some of their fondest
memories from childhood and committed to including these in
their parenting life. When their kids were two and five years
old, Jon and Jess met for the first time with a parenting coach.
Jon wanted established bedtimes; Jess felt they should allow
the kids to sleep when they were ready. Jess wanted more time
for fun and exploration, Jon wanted to know whether he could
plan anything else on a Saturday or if the entire day would be
dedicated to "family fun." With new strategies in hand and a
commitment to work together to implement them, life improved
for a few years until both kids entered school. As time went on,
it became clear that Jess and Jon were unable to co-parent on
even the simplest issues. The disagreements on bedtimes and
sleep turned into resentments about each other that burrowed
deep and became the foundation for their daily interactions. In
hopes of saving their marriage, Jon and Jess visited a marriage
counselor for guidance.

Margo and Steven worked with a couple's counselor early
on in their marriage and learned valuable techniques to help
them communicate better and to be more accepting and encouraging of each other. But this did nothing to improve their ability
to co-parent effectively. "Steven wanted our kids to have a full
social life with lots of extracurricular activities, and I thought

we were pushing them too fast and too far too early. We used all the techniques we learned in counseling to work our way through this issue and in spite of our best attempts we were still at an impasse. It isn't that he is more social, or that I don't want the kids to be involved in life; it's that we don't share the same attitudes or beliefs regarding this subject. Until we were able to explore our childhood experiences and pinpoint the reason we developed these very personal and specific beliefs, we were stuck. No one tells you how many issues there will be along your parenting journey. We all think that an initial conversation is enough to prepare us for co-parenting. We don't know what we don't know."

Many couples say they experience some level of success when working with a parenting coach, but it's usually a specific child related challenge that gets addressed, and so they experience positive change in this one area. And many parents report a deeper level of satisfaction and happiness in their marriage after working with a marriage professional, but this doesn't extend into their co-parenting life. Having a strong marriage and having solid parenting strategies is not enough to successfully negotiate the tricky terrain of co-parenting with someone who has an entirely different idea on how to raise the kids.

After a couple commits the time and money in working with a parenting coach or a marriage counselor, it's tough to accept that you still can't make your co-parenting life work. If you are already feeling discouraged about the way you are co-parenting and working with an expert doesn't provide any relief, the discouragement can cause further damage to the marriage and the family as a whole.

With few resources available on how to work together harmoniously as a collective team, dissension grows and families are fractured. I don't think it occurred to anyone that once dad became an equal partner in the raising of the kids, it might have been wise to take a moment and pause to consider this new family dynamic and the impact of a parenting team rather than a primary caregiver on family life. I can say without hesitation that the parents I worked and talked with did the best they could with the information they had. In some cases parents may have taken the time to communicate their desires and flush out areas where they might be in disagreement, but in many cases a quick *this is going to be great, we are in this together, rah, rah* attitude was all the consideration and collaboration this new dynamic was given.

In every situation that requires us to make a parenting decision there is the potential for one or both parents to be triggered and that can activate an entire range of emotions and responses. Working from different perspectives on how to raise the kids manifests as an inability to work together and make unified parenting decisions in the best interest of their children.

I firmly believe that couples are using all their available resources to help them in their co-parenting lives, but it can be difficult to accurately interpret the beliefs, attitudes and values of your partner and then merge them with yours into one clear cohesive plan without a model for communication and collaboration.

Influencing Childhood Experiences

Each one of us experienced our childhood in unique and profoundly personal ways, and through these experiences we developed a specific set of beliefs, attitudes, preferences and values. In other words, we each have our own set of goggles through which we view ourselves, others and the world around us. Each of us has our own beliefs about who we are and how we belong, what is important in life and how we want to raise our children. Oftentimes our goggles are blinders to the views of others, and it is difficult to see life from another perspective, especially when that other perspective is in direct opposition to ours. This is especially true when it comes to parenting. Unknowingly we begin making major life decisions during our own adolescence about the kind of parent we want to be and over time, these decisions become the beliefs that guide our every parenting decision. Imagine the complexity of parenting when there are two individuals, with not just different ideas on parenting but a set of concrete beliefs on a subject that they know little or nothing about, and who have not taken the time to flush out where they might intersect in their desires and where they undoubtedly diverge. It's easy to see why a chain reaction of frustration, misunderstanding and anger can erupt, leaving each parent confused, misunderstood and feeling judged and unheard.

Even the parents I talked with who went beyond the initial "I don't believe in spanking!"; "Let's never fight in front of the kids!"; or "I will always have your back" conversations found themselves struggling to overcome their differences and couldn't express why they were so stuck—just that they were. Few of them could articulate where the breakdown in their marriage and parenting life was coming from and even more frustrating to them was how to get beyond it. This was true for the parents who worked with a parenting coach and/or a marriage therapist. There was initial improvement in a particular challenge with a child or in their life as a couple, but it did not address the couple's inability to co-parent successfully. All of this can only be explained when we understand that our past childhood experiences are driving our present day parenting decisions.

Have you ever heard yourself speaking to your child and knew with alarming certainty that the words you were using were the same your parents used with you? It can be a rude awakening to realize that we are more like our parents than we first imagined, and that although we may have promised that we would never speak to our kids in a particular way, we are doing just that. It is proof, like it or not, that we are deeply influenced by our childhood experiences and why it is so important to understand how those experiences developed into beliefs, values and attitudes that influence our everyday parenting decisions. As if untangling and understanding your own childhood wasn't confusing enough, consider that your partner has his or her own set of experiences, and along with them, the beliefs, values and attitudes which guide their parenting decisions. It's no wonder co-parenting is challenging even when the couple has taken the time to talk about their childhood experiences. It isn't until our children arrive that we truly begin to understand the complicated nature of co-parenting.

Recreate or Reject

Dr. Frank Walton is a renowned Adlerian psychologist whose work in the field of family dynamics is legendary. One of the significant contributions to the practice of Adlerian counseling and therapy in recent years was creation of a powerful technique known as "The Most Memorable Observation" (see http://www.drfrankwalton.com for more details). He uses this exercise to help parents pinpoint some of the decisions they may have made during childhood that impact their parenting attitudes, skills and decisions.

> Sometime in our early teenage years, or even in late preteen years, it seems very common for each of us to look around our family life and draw a conclusion about some aspect of life that appears to be important. Sometimes it is positive, "I really like this aspect of life in our family. When I get to be an adult I'd like it to be just this way in my own family." Often it is negative, "I don't like this at all. This is really distasteful. When I get to be an adult I am going to do everything I can to keep this from occurring in my family." What was it for you? As you think of life in your family about age 11, 12, 13 or so, what conclusion do you think you drew? It may have been positive, it may have been negative, or it may have been both.
>
> (Walton 2016)

It is likely that when you were between ten and thirteen, you observed your family and identified specific experiences that you wished to recreate with your own children. Perhaps you can think of a few right now and you see their influence in your current parenting approach.

It's important to clarify that it's not so much the experience itself but the meaning we ascribe to the experience that's important. For instance, Marjorie recalls coming home from school each day to a kitchen that smelled of warm cookies and a mother waiting to greet her. She felt loved, cared for and believed her mother was interested in her as a person, and she wants to recreate that feeling with her own kids. If she isn't clear that it's the feelings of connection, love and acceptance she is trying to recreate with her kids, rather than having home baked cookies ready when her kids arrive home, any negative feedback, criticism or opposition to her making cookies for the kids from her partner is likely to activate a strong reaction from her. Imagine her response if one of her children suddenly announces that she isn't interested in cookies or answering her mother's questions about her day at school. You can almost hear the rip in the relationship just thinking about this exchange. In recognizing that her goal is not the cookies but the feeling of being loved unconditionally she is trying to recreate, she can look for new ways to create situations that will become her children's memories, rather than trying to recreate her own childhood.

Like Marjorie, many parents try to recreate with their children the positive experiences from their own childhood but get stuck in trying to replicate the details rather than on capturing the feeling and meaning of the experience. This is a recipe for disaster if the other parent has opposing beliefs associated with these experiences. It's easy for each partner to jump to conclusions and become defensive and critical. With emotions running hot and high, it leaves little room for discussion at the time of the misunderstanding and that in turn leads to resentments that build over time.

Here is an example:

Susan wants to ensure her kids have a hot breakfast before they go to school because her father worked nights and couldn't have dinner with the family and instead made sure to spend quality time with his children during breakfast. She associates this gesture with love and connection, and attributes her love of school to the morning ritual. This wouldn't be a problem if her partner Kevin had the same childhood experience as Susan, but he didn't. He remembers many occasions when his mother fussed over him at breakfast, making him feel like a baby, and it was worse when he had friends over and he felt embarrassed by her treatment of him. Each time he sees Susan "fussing" over the kids, his childhood memory is activated and he feels that same embarrassment he felt as a kid. His knee-jerk reaction is to make snide remarks that activate Susan's defenses. Until Kevin and Susan are able to identify the meaning they have ascribed to this simple situation, this seemingly inconsequential event has the power to fracture their parenting relationship and impact the family in decidedly negative ways.

Kevin reflects, "As soon as I started to hear Susan's story, I could understand why making breakfast for the kids was important to her. When she heard my story her eyes filled with tears. She understood immediately what it must have been like for me as a kid. We talked about how we could modify the mornings so that we could both connect with the kids before we headed out for the day and create a balance between Susan cooking for the kids and the kids taking on more responsibility. There is a whole new energy during breakfast, and this success has made it possible for us to explore other areas of our co-parenting life with enthusiasm rather than dread." To continue with Dr. Walton's exercise, it's also possible that you looked around your family and identified experiences that you found unpleasant and do not want to recreate with your own children.

For example, Dan's parents forced him into playing sports he wasn't interested in and pursue theater as a solution to his introvert personality. He was not an especially gifted athlete and spent more time on the bench than he ever did on the field. Likewise, he worked on lighting and set design, rather than spending any time on stage. Dan resented the way his parents pushed him, and felt that they discounted and disrespected him as a person with his own interests and would often criticize his suggestions for extracurricular activities he might like to try. Dan decided he would never force his kids into any sports or activities they didn't seem genuinely interested in, and would support any and all activities the kids wanted to explore.

Like Dan, Cheryl's parents forced her to play sports and signed her up for every camp their local recreation center offered, but unlike Dan, she associated their actions with love and interest in her. She attributes her deep sense of confidence and outgoing nature to their pushing her, and says it was the reason she got a full scholarship to college and met some of her best friends. She wanted to do the same for her kids.

Cheryl misunderstood Dan's reasons for refusing to push their kids to try new things, and why he allowed them to quit after they signed up for a sport they thought they might like. It was a point of contention in their parenting life, and it spilled over into their marriage, which was quickly unraveling.

"I knew Dan's parents pushed him, but I didn't understand that it left him feeling completely discounted, dismissed and disrespected by them. My feelings run in the opposite direction. I associate my memories with my parents believing in me and my abilities as them wanting me to believe in myself in the same way they believed in me. Instead of talking about our childhoods, we focused on what we wanted for our kids, and it turns out we want exactly the same thing. To introduce our kids to new things, support them as they figure out what they like to do and then help them through the times when they want to throw in the towel and quit. We even figured out who would talk to the kids at what times. I am the parent they need when they are ready to quit, and Dan is the parent they need when they are exploring their options." Exploring your childhood experiences and having your partner do the same will help you gain valuable insight and provide the clarity that is necessary to design and then implement your own co-parenting plan.

Perhaps you were given this book as a baby shower gift, maybe you and your partner are proactive by nature, maybe you have seen firsthand how other couples argue and struggle around their child-raising methods, and maybe you are that couple that is merely cohabiting at this stage in your relationship because the stress and strain of co-parenting has made you adversaries rather than allies. In any case, my goal is to offer you a chance to use this book to look back at your childhoods, create a model for collaboration and show up together to one of the most rewarding and fulfilling experiences life has to offer, with an appreciation for each other and a plan that will guide you through all the parenting decisions you will make as you raise your children from infancy to young adulthood.

Bibliography

Dell'Antonia, K.J. "Well Family: A New Name and New Home for Motherlode." *New York Times Parenting Blogs*, accessed March 3, 2016, http://parenting.blogs.nytimes.com/2016/03/03/well-family-a-new-name-and-new-home-for-motherlode/

Walton, F.X. "Most Memorable Observation." *Dr Frank Walton*, accessed January, 2016, http://drfrankwalton.com/wp-content/uploads/2016/01/mostmemobservcorr.pdf

2

Planning for Your Partnership

For you and your partner to co-parent successfully through every age and stage of your children's lives, a well thought out parenting plan and a set of skills to help you navigate the process of creating that plan initially is required. Then you are charged with the challenge of sticking to this plan over time with respect, openness and honesty for yourself and your partner. This is your opportunity to set the stage for success and explore areas that will have a direct impact on your ability to work collaboratively with your partner in designing and then implementing your parenting plan. Some of these areas are between you and your partner; some come at the unwittingly crafty hand of your children and others from the looks of unsuspecting friends or bystanders. Taking the time to identify them, before you are knee-deep in the middle of a conversation or floored by a response to something you said or did, will go a long way in pushing through and achieving the original and planned outcome.

Communication

Whether we know it or not, we are always communicating either by our attitude, words or actions (and our kids are watching and learning). Most parents I talk with say they are good, clear, strong, respectful communicators. And they are, when they have had enough rest, enough caffeine, enough yoga, enough sex, enough alone time, enough of whatever the thing is that grounds and centers them. When there hasn't been enough of what we need to remain in balance, communication suffers, and for this reason, I bring it up here. Lousy communication is enough to undo any of the work you and your partner put into completing the exercises in this book. No matter how good we think we are at communicating, a small gesture, a tone, a roll of the eyes, or a dismissive *tsk* can end any potentially productive conversation immediately and definitively. Here is a chance for you to take an honest inventory of how you communicate, not only when you are at your best, but when you feel angry, disrespected, ignored, overlooked, threatened or hurt. Admitting that you aren't always the best communicator when you are experiencing a negative emotion opens the door for learning new and more effective ways of talking and listening during difficult moments. The following are specific examples of how our messages misfire, and we fall into ineffective communication habits.

Passive Aggressive Messages

Remarks like "It's fine" or "I don't care" or "Do whatever you want" send a very clear message that in fact you do care, you do have an opinion and it isn't fine at all. This passive aggressive communication style, when used as a fall back method to end a discussion (or argument) with your partner, instead of remaining calm and articulating what you believe, want or need, causes resentment and unnecessary misunderstandings.

Sharon recalls, "My go-to is *do whatever you want, it's not that important to me*, which is a lie. I throw it at my partner to let him know I'm pissed and to hurt him because I feel hurt. This is especially true when it comes to our parenting. To make things worse, I walk away, sulk and instead of having one problem to solve, we have multiple problems to weed through, and because we are fairly certain each conversation will end in the same way, we try and avoid them altogether. We both end up harboring resentments toward the other, and that interferes with our ability to co-parent successfully."

This communication style is a power play disguised as submission. Instead of walking straight into the snare, try taking a deep breath and mustering up a bit of courage to share your idea, your concern, your perspective or to ask for what you want. It may seem awkward at first, but if you give yourself time to practice and you ask your partner for assistance as you break this pesky habit, you will find yourself feeling more confident sharing what is on your mind, in the moment, in a respectful and productive way.

Don't *Should* on Me

Most of us have heard the expression *don't should on me*, and yet we still do a great deal of *shoulding* on ourselves and others on a regular basis. The word *should* is one of the most highly charged and disempowering words in the English language, and it is a word thrown around quite loosely.

Statements like "I really should turn off the television and go to bed" activate feelings of guilt if we don't actually turn the television off and go to bed. That guilt turns to resentment, stubbornness or discouragement toward ourselves. These negative feelings and judgments then filter out and land on those we feel closest to—namely, our kids and partner.

Statements like "I don't think you should do that," said to your partner, are another way of saying, "I don't think you have what it takes to make a decision for yourself, so I will tell you what to do," which again leads to resentment and distance.

No matter how or when it's used, the word itself interferes with respectful, honest and effective communication and can send a conversation spiraling out of control in a matter of minutes.

One client recalled her powerful insight after we explored the word should in her life: "My partner and I were able to identify an area of life where we intersected and were really excited to create our first parenting plan together. After years of my husband feeling judged and feeling disappointed myself, we were looking forward to working together for the good of our family. Imagine our surprise when our plan not only didn't work, but made things worse between the two of us. It turns out that I had an entire belief system developed that was based on *shoulds*. Good mothers *should*, good fathers *should*, good kids *should*. *Shoulds* were running and ruining my life, and they trumped the wonderful parenting plan my partner and I created together. Now, when I hear myself thinking, *I should or he should or they should*, I reframe it and suddenly all kinds of options open up to me that I never would have considered before."

Try replacing the word *should* with:

- ◆ Next time I could. . .
- ◆ Next time I will try. . .
- ◆ What could I have done differently?
- ◆ Are you open to. . .

Discouraging or Encouraging Language

Most of us have some understanding of the difference between discouraging and encouraging words, and the power each of them have to either lift us up or tear us down. We are a culture committed to pointing out the worst, in ourselves and in others. In spite of all the research that suggests that people do not do better when they are made to feel badly, discouraging and disempowering words are littered throughout our daily conversations. When we take the time to listen to the language we use and then commit to using more uplifting language, it becomes possible to change the atmosphere in your home from tense and trying to happy and harmonious.

Here is a brief list I have generated over the years of discouraging or disempowering words or phrases and their encouraging or empowering counterparts. It might be interesting, if not fun, for you to keep track of how often you use each set of words in your own life, both with yourself and with your spouse and kids. After you identify the biggest offenders, pick one or two that you will intentionally replace with the word from the empowering list, and practice until the new word has replaced the disempowering word in your vocabulary.

Encouraging

How are you feeling? Yes. Wow. Enjoy. That works for me. What happens if we? I am interested in hearing more. I need your help. This is our time. Terrific. That is a help.

I hear you. Let's try together. That's great. I'm glad you're here. We all make mistakes.

Thank you. Remember when? I love you. What is your plan? You really helped me.

Discouraging

Not like that. No. You don't need to get upset. You aren't listening to me. When will you learn?

I can do this without your help. It's about time. You never. You should. You never learn. That was stupid. You didn't give that much thought. It is easier if I do it myself. You are wrong.

You don't listen. How many times to do I have to tell you?

Identify and Anchor

I have also found it helpful to incorporate the use of character traits or qualities we admire in others into our daily communication with those closest to us. If we want to bring out the best in ourselves and others, then it makes sense that we acknowledge when someone is being their best self. You observe or identify the character trait and anchor it with the experience.

Here are a few examples of this strategy.

Partner to Partner

"I know you were disappointed when Jane decided not to go to the store with you, and I appreciate your willingness to reach out and ask her to join you at the park."

"I appreciate how respectful you were talking to Jack, even though he was clearly trying to provoke you by being blatantly disrespectful."

"I can understand that being patient while Lindsay learns to load the dishwasher takes all your willpower, but seeing the look on your faces when she finished was something to behold."

"I could see how furious you were with Annie when she lashed out at you, and yet your compassion was evident when she finally told us what was really going on."

"I appreciate how truly angry you were when Tony took the car without asking, and that you chose to treat him with respect and dignity as you figured out a solution."

Parent to Child

"I appreciate how hard it was to leave the party. You handled yourself with grace and demonstrated courage by walking away."

"It takes a lot of courage to arrange a meeting with a teacher that scares you, and yet you didn't miss a beat. You recognized what you needed to communicate, you created the opportunity to do so, you respectfully shared your thoughts, and you facilitated change."

"Your kindness and patience toward your grandfather as you listen to his detailed stories for the twentieth time fills me with love. You inspire me to be present when he and I visit."

"You showed so much flexibility when we had to change our plans from the park to the bowling alley. I know that you had your heart set on mastering the swing-set, but you were willing to consider your cousin's preference."

The language we use creates an environment rich in love, acceptance, compassion, thoughtfulness and respect, or it doesn't. We are the masters of the language we use, and it is never too late to teach ourselves how to focus on the positive and replace negative, disempowering, hurtful words with words that encourage and inspire.

The Blame Game

Daniel and Eliot

"My parents had incredibly high expectations of me when I was a kid. Not only that, they thought a child who made a mistake was a reflection of their parenting, so mistakes were something to avoid. I once heard Vicki say that kids who avoid taking responsibility for their mistakes and who blame other people or circumstances lack the courage to step up and own what they have done. That is me. I am a blamer. I am so afraid of owning my mistakes for fear of disappointing someone or being downright rejected by them, that I point the finger as quickly as I can to avoid any chance someone will find out I messed up. You can imagine how this plays out in my parenting life. I have to be right all the time or I point the finger at my kids or my partner and start a fight rather than admitting my error and spending time figuring out a solution. Of course the other downside of this trait is that my kids have been watching me avoid responsibility and now they think this is an option for them. You would think I would be understanding, but just the opposite is true. When they try and blame someone else or deny they made the mistake, I come unglued and berate them the way my parents did me. This enrages my partner, who then attacks me for having a double standard. He is right, of course; I do have a double standard. The only way out of this nightmare was to get really clear about those messages and the beliefs I adopted and instead of beating myself up, create new, healthier beliefs. Over time, I have found the courage I need to own my mistakes, and each time I do, I am rewarded with that feeling inside that tells me I am moving in the right direction."

Many of us grew up in households where mistakes were not opportunities for learning, but rather opportunities for lectures, criticism, scolding and punishment. It's no wonder many of us looked to avoid making mistakes altogether, and when we did make them, we pointed the finger out toward someone or something rather than at ourselves. It takes courage to own your mistakes, and this can be difficult for many parents. There is this assumption that we should know what we are doing by the time we have kids, but if you have kids, you already know that we rarely have any idea what we are doing, so mistakes are a part of daily life. It's true that by the time the kids hit the school years, we have figured a few things out, but I can tell you, I am still apologizing to my oldest daughter (who is now twenty-seven years old), because everything is a first with her, which means I continue to make mistakes. Thankfully, she is very forgiving, and as long as I come clean with my mess-up, she is willing to let me off the hook.

At the heart of it, the blame game is about vulnerability and uncertainty. With practice, patience and honesty, you and your parenting partner can steer clear of the blame game and focus your attention on accepting responsibility for what is yours, learning from your mistakes and creating a plan for moving forward.

Breaking the cycle of shame, blame, judgment and criticism starts with us, with you; it starts now and it's as simple as stepping up and taking responsibility for what is yours.

Here are three things you can do to break the cycle of blame and learn to communicate more honestly, openly and effectively:

1. If blaming others is a sign that you lack courage, what one thing could you do in this situation that would make you feel more courageous?
2. Tweeze apart your story and identify what you are afraid of or what is holding you back by filling in the blanks in the following statement. I believe that if I admit I did (blank), you will (blank), and that makes me (blank).

For instance, I believe that if I admit I forgot to tell the kids we were leaving at 6:00 p.m., you will think I am stupid and irresponsible, and that makes me question myself as a parent.

Create a family culture that focuses on solutions rather than on identifying problems and assigning blame. When you create a solution based atmosphere within the family, everyone feels more confident admitting to mistakes and taking responsibility for them.

I encourage you to enter into every conversation with a sense of humility and your attention firmly fixed on how you are communicating, rather than on how your partner is communicating. When you feel yourself getting heated, stop, take a breath and ask for clarification. If you find yourself feeling guarded or defensive, stop and state clearly what you are feeling without blaming anyone for the feeling. If you allow emotions to settle for just a few moments, they will either dissolve altogether or offer you a glimpse into what might be triggering your response. Again, if you aren't willing to do this for yourself, your spouse or your relationship, pause for a moment and imagine how helpful it will be for your kids to watch you take responsibility for yourself in potentially high-stake moments, and maybe that's enough to motivate you to take the time and put in the effort in this essential area of co-parenting. Think about it for a minute.

Communication is the execution of your plan. If you sabotage this step, it will undo all the time and effort you put into creating the plan in the first place.

Trip-Ups of Life

After flushing out your memories which fostered a belief system that is influencing your parenting decisions today, there is still the matter of your children's responses to your parenting decisions, or as I prefer to call them, life's little trip-ups, that have the potential to derail any progress you and your partner hope to make in executing your parenting plan. Here are a few common trip-up stories to illustrate the power these rascals have to undo your good intentions. Remember, you are looking to expose any and all of them before the fact, so you aren't caught unaware the next time they make an untimely appearance.

Emotional Responses to Discipline

If you have dedicated time to create a cohesive, fair and respectful plan for discipline, which of these common trip-ups has the potential to undo all of your hard work?

- ♦ A child who says "I hate you" or says you are mean and runs to the other parent for comfort
- ♦ A child who sobs uncontrollably
- ♦ A child whose behavior doesn't change immediately
- ♦ A partner who doesn't follow through and gives in to the child
- ♦ A partner who starts yelling because they lose patience with you or the child
- ♦ Judgment from family, friends, or strangers on your strategy

These are just a few of the trip-ups that can undo a carefully crafted plan especially when we consider that (1) most parents would rather not discipline at all and hope they have a child who will hear their explanation, nod their head in compliance and follow their parents' wishes, and (2) you may know what outcome you want, but haven't thought about what it will take for your child to actually develop the long-term behavior you are looking for. After all, no one changes overnight or the diet and fitness industry wouldn't be where it is today.

Anger

"We found where we intersected easily, and we agreed on a plan for how we could best support each other and the kids in an area where we struggled a bit as a family. The eye opener was when we talked about what trips us up. Wow. How did we not know this about each other? As it turns out I become undone when one of the kids is angry with me and gives me the silent treatment. I will back pedal on a decision my partner and I made together, which completely undermines him. When we discovered this, it was like someone turned the light bulb on and we could pinpoint all the times our best laid plans were unraveled by these sneaky villains. It was as simple as my partner saying to me, 'What can I do to support you when the kids get angry with you and give you the silent treatment?' I felt immediately supported, understood and empowered. We decided that initially I would leave the room and he would take over. Fast forward a few months, and now those trip-ups are no longer holding me hostage. In fact, this insight allowed me to talk honestly with the kids about how they used their anger and their silent treatment in unhealthy ways. As a result, we have all improved when it comes to owning our anger and not using it against those we love."

Crying and Begging

Your childhood impressions revealed your decision to establish bedtime routines with your own children. This decision is supported by your belief that good parents enforce established bedtimes aimed at providing enough sleep, so children can function during their day at home or school. Here is one possible trip-up sure to derail your best laid plans. Your children cry and beg you to stay with them until they fall asleep, and this gets you wondering if you are being a bad parent by holding to your routine. You find yourself getting impatient and short with your children, which sends them spiraling into a meltdown that ends with you snuggled up in bed with them until they fall asleep. Not exactly what you had in mind when you designed your plan. To make matters worse, your partner is waiting downstairs so you can have a serious discussion about a problem at work. Consider whether your reaction to the crying is in alignment with your goal of an established bedtime routine, or if you are giving in to your idea that you might be a bad parent if your children get upset and resort to crying and begging. Can you see how this trip-up might show up when it's time for you to leave the park, or when you say no to an extra cookie, or if you take a toy away after it's been thrown?

Eternally Indecisive

You want your kids to eat a well-balanced breakfast and will ensure they get one before they leave for school. Your trip-up might be the child who asks for a bagel and then refuses to eat it, because it is too brown. Will your desire to send them off with a balanced breakfast mean that you will make them multiple meals if they ask? If you do, are you likely to build up a bit of resentment if this habit continues? If your goal is to ensure they have a healthy breakfast, is there another way to accomplish this that doesn't include you being the short order cook? This same trip-up could rear its ugly head when your child decides to change her clothes right before you leave for church or when he decides he doesn't like the lunch you packed and asks you to start again. It's a sure bet that if you are focused on the outcome rather than employing your parenting strategy to facilitate learning, this trip-up will find multiple entry points into your life, so be on the lookout.

Peer Parent Pressure

John and Sarah agreed that they would not coax their child into toilet-training when the time came. Instead, when the time seemed right, they would allow their child to go naked on the weekends as a way to promote natural toilet-training. At around two-years-old, their son, Max, began to show signs that he was ready to use the toilet. They executed their plan and allowed him to remain naked during the weekend, knowing that there could be accidents and that it could take several weeks before Max would be completely trained to use the toilet. They were ready for this and even said that they felt like warriors taking this jumbo sized job on together.

Unexpectedly, friends from college called to say they would be in town for a few days and would love to spend time with them. John and Sarah agreed and invited their friends over for an extended day visit. Without warning, Max entered the room in a diaper and what Sarah described as "the outfit he wears when his grandparents visit." Not only was Sarah shocked to see her son dressed; her son was none-too-happy about the sudden need for clothing and kept trying to remove the diaper. When that didn't work, he would fall apart, which quickly turned to a full on meltdown.

After their guests left, Sarah asked John what happened, and John immediately began to defend his decision to put Max in diapers for the day. When Sarah pressed him, he had no real answer for her other than to say, "It shouldn't matter why I did it. I am Max's parent and even though we had an agreement, it shouldn't be any big deal that I made a parenting decision in the moment."

Sarah later confessed that she wasn't even that upset about seeing Max fully dressed, but she was shocked at how defensive John became when she questioned him.

As we talked, John revealed that when he was a kid growing up, his mom made most of his clothes. "I always felt like such a," he paused searching for a word from his past, "goober growing up. The kids laughed at me daily. My mom was very cavalier about the whole thing and said for me not to worry about what other kids said. Easy for her to say. She didn't have to endure the daily humiliation. Later, I found out that she made all my clothes so she could brag to her friends. Here she was telling me not to be influenced by what others thought of me, and yet she was making decisions for exactly the same thing—to impress her friends. I didn't realize how much pressure I put on myself to act as if what others think of me doesn't matter, when in fact it matters a lot to me." What tripped Max up was his fear of being judged by other people.

With this new insight, Sarah and John are in a position to talk through some of the other areas where they are bound to feel judged by friends, family and even strangers. They will both have to decide where their individual thresholds are and respect that they may be very different. By acknowledging his belief, John is in a position to identify when he gets activated and work with Sarah to shift his perspective and stay on the course he and Sarah mapped out together.

Sarah shared, "We came up with a quick code to help us navigate this area of our parenting. I would say to John when I saw him getting agitated, 'Us or them?'" Most of the time, John would say "us," and they could enforce a decision they made together as a couple. Sometimes it was too much for him, and in those moments Sarah was willing to support him and let it go. This give and take felt to them, like a true partnership.

These are just a few of the hundreds of stories shared by parents who identified their trip-ups. No doubt you will stumble upon your own, and when you do (you will feel a very strong almost indescribable emotion or you will totally abandon the agreement you made with your parenting partner), take a moment and examine how often those trip-ups are the reason you and your partner might be struggling to connect, agree and work toward co-parenting with respect and love.

The Impact on Children

I'm including this section here rather than at the end of the book because you might be thinking this is going to be difficult and wonder, *What difference does it all make anyway?* This might be the motivation you need to keep going. Consider that your children are watching you and all of the interactions between you and your partner, and as they do, they begin to construct a very personal relationship blueprint based on not only your relationship with them as your child, but just as importantly, the relationship they see between you and your partner. Consider the messages you may be sending to the kids when the two of you work against each other rather than with each other. How you work together is more influential than how each of you works individually.

Ask yourself, would you want your son or daughter's partner talking to your child the way you are speaking to your partner, or vice versa? If not, then it's time to take this entire co-parenting plan seriously.

Illustrating the Impact
Here are just a few quick stories that I have gathered over the years from parents who were willing to share their experiences with me.

Sarcasm Stings
"We got a wake-up call from a friend who, after hearing us complain about how sarcastic our daughter was when she didn't get her own way, told us, in no uncertain terms, 'She sounds exactly like the two of you when you are at odds with each other.' How had we not seen this, or rather heard this? We thought the sarcasm was over her head, but obviously she was not only observing; she was mimicking what she was hearing."

Always a Skeptic
"The first time we heard our daughter say to her sister, 'Oh right, like that will work,' we knew something had to change."

Manipulation
"The other night my son and his girlfriend were trying to work out vacation plans. He wanted her to ask for time off from work, and she was nervous to ask. He started pouting and withdrawing when she didn't immediately agree. I saw my own problem solving skills (or lack thereof) in my son. It was painfully obvious that he was mimicking my behavior of trying to manipulate my wife in order to get my own way. They watch, they learn and then they do."

Dismissive Diva
"My husband and I are finally on the same page, but this was after years of battle. Unfortunately, I am recognizing that my daughters dismiss their dad on a regular basis and I realize they

learned this from watching me. When he said something I didn't like or agree with, I dismissed his very idea, and I am ashamed to say, sometimes I dismissed him. It was a coping mechanism, so I could avoid getting upset, but it also ensured we never got around to solving our problems. I have learned to reframe my old beliefs, so that I don't dismiss or avoid, but it's clear that I will have to help my daughters learn new and better problem solving skills. You don't realize how much of an impact your co-parenting life has on your kids until you see yourself in them, and then the truth is impossible to overlook."

Peace and Joy

"I am the mother of five active children and I love my busy life, but I am a consummate conflict avoider. Until now, my husband has been willing to step up and handle most of the conflict in the house, but in the process he has been labeled the 'mean parent,' while I have been labeled the 'nice mommy.' We are working to create more balance in this area, but the impact on our kids can't be ignored. Our oldest daughter who is entering middle school has learned from me that conflict is something to be avoided, and this translates into her friendships, and recently with a boyfriend. We heard the boy say he wanted to do something that we know our daughter has no interest in, but she gave in when he raised his voice. My husband and I recognized our roles immediately. It was gut wrenching. As my husband and I continue to create new and healthier beliefs and habits, we have to teach our children what we are learning, so they can incorporate it into their lives."

In Command

"I like order. I am constantly directing my husband and children. I have three children: one who waits to be directed and the other two who are so inflexible with each other that we can't plan a simple meal. It pains me to see the two oldest treat each other so disrespectfully, but I know where they learned it. It is time for me to zip it and spend time supporting them as they develop new skills."

One of my clients, a scientist, claimed that our thoughts traveled faster than our words. When it comes to communicating with our children and our partners, I believe him. Becoming more aware of our communication patterns is the first step in becoming an effective communicator. Listen to your words, your tone and your volume, and watch your attitude and body language for clues that will help you make small adjustments. The way you are communicating with your spouse and your children is the blueprint for how your children will communicate with their world. Take the time to check yourself and model for your children a method of communicating that will serve them well in the future. If this all sounds foreign to you and you have no idea what is bubbling below the surface of your actions, reactions and responses, the next section of the book is going to guide you on this journey of self-discovery.

Part I
Self-Discovery/Discovery

3

Childhood Experiences Revisited

Pam and Scott have been married for twelve years. They have three children. They both agree that when they are away together it is bliss, but when the kids and their roles as parents are added to the mix, they hardly recognize the other.

Pam says, "I have read my share of how-tos on maintaining a healthy marriage while raising kids and I have read parenting books, parenting blogs and attended a few workshops on how to be a good parent and raise great kids, and in spite of that, we have trouble merging our parenting perspectives in order to make unified decisions for our kids. We know we are supposed to listen and to affirm each other and a host of other great ideas, and we do that. But when we hit one of the trigger spots, like whether or not it's okay to let the kids go to school without their backpack and experience a natural consequence, we both dig in our heels, run to our corners, come out fighting to prove our way of thinking is right and prepared to win the battle. We are brutal with each other and our kids are witnessing this blood bath. It has to stop, but I have no idea how to break this toxic cycle."

Pam and Scott represent many parents who each believe they know what is best for their kids. Tensions arise between the couple when what one parent believes is best is in conflict with what their partner believes is best. With so few resources to guide a couple through the treacherous territory of successful co-parenting, they are left to figure things out on their own, which typically includes conversations riddled with *yeah buts* and *you don't understands* and, eventually, a *fine, do what you want*. As they each hold to their beliefs, attitudes, values and perspectives which often do not align with their partner's, they face the difficult, if not downright daunting task of trying to make a unified parenting decision they can both stand behind.

The very techniques that can help a couple develop a strong marriage and the strategies to help deal with sibling rivalry or messy bedrooms are not the same strategies or techniques required if their goal is to arrive at a place where they are capable of actually creating and then executing a co-parenting plan together. In my experience, in order for the couple to co-parent successfully, they will need to:

1. Identify their strongest childhood experiences and determine whether they are trying to recreate them or reject them altogether.
2. Accept that their partner has strong childhood experiences that he or she wants to recreate or reject, and that in order to co-create a parenting plan that will work for everyone, they will both have to take each other's desires into account.
3. Accept that there is no absolute way to raise healthy kids. Remaining flexible and open-minded when working with your partner will mean the difference between failure and success, and yes, I am saying that if things go south from here you will have to take responsibility for that.

The book is designed and organized to make it simple for you and your partner to examine your own childhood experiences, and understand how those experiences became concrete beliefs about the best way to raise children and how those beliefs are influencing your parenting decisions of today. Once you both have a better understanding of your decision making process, you are in a position to work together in an atmosphere of cooperation, support and open-mindedness, with a goal to co-parent in the best interest of your children. Creating a shared vision along with a solid parenting plan will ensure that you enjoy years of successful co-parenting and that no one is worried about being ejected from the equation.

Refer to this book during any stage of your child's life and revisit it when you find yourself at odds with your partner for no discernable reason. It will address often overlooked areas that cause strife between parents, as well as the obvious pain points that lead to disagreements, dissension and resentment. Be patient with the process. This isn't a race. With time, you will begin to see patterns emerge and with them new possibilities for working together to create a parenting plan that you both feel good about executing. You will also begin to notice that with each bit of progress and improvement in one area of your co-parenting life, you begin to see other areas mysteriously resolve themselves. This is common in my work. It's called the layering effect.

Chapter 4 focuses your attention on the different relationships within your family structure, including the relationship you have with each of your parents, the relationship between your parents in their roles as parenting partners, your relationship with your siblings, as well as a section on friendships. Don't worry, this isn't therapy and you won't be required to expose any more than you are comfortable exploring with your partner when the time comes. It is an opportunity for you to examine those relationships and gather information that will help you parent from your best and work cooperatively with your partner.

Chapter 5 focuses on the day-to-day operations in your family—everything from manners to the use of technology. This area of life is where many parents make on-the-spot decisions that are more reactionary than responsive, and we are notorious for changing our decisions from one day to the next: "Yes you may have dessert tonight even though we have a policy that dessert is only for the weekends." These on-the-spot decisions often overlook our partner's wishes, and if they aren't there to represent themselves, they are given no consideration at all. This perceived lack of consideration and blatant disrespect can lead to tiny fractures in our co-parenting life, which can become a breeding ground for mistrust and resentments. It's also an easy place to start our journey together as a co-parenting team.

Chapter 6 is dedicated to what I call *lifestyles*: areas of life including independence, discipline, education and religion. It is here that we can often experience stress with our partner without the ability to clearly articulate where the stress is coming from. It's easy to make generalizations—for instance, you might state, "I want to foster my child's independence," but without considering what that means to each of you and then finding a way to implement your ideas so that they take into account the children you are living with, the statement can cause conflict rather than cooperation.

Each chapter will bring you deeper into your childhood experience and allow you to discover decisions you made that are influencing your current parenting practices. This is a time of exploration, and it can be exciting and rewarding to finally understand an area of life with your partner and your kids that has been challenging and upsetting when you realize that a resolution is only moments away. Each chapter is slightly different, so as to keep your brain engaged and the memories flowing easily. Exploring every aspect of childhood would be impossible, so I have done my best to address the most common areas of conflict, as well as the areas that are often overlooked until we are knee-deep in frustration and resentment, and coming to resolution seems near impossible. At the end of each chapter, you will find additional topics that you can explore on your own using the same format.

Navigating the Book

In Part I you will find two exercises designed to trigger memories that will lead you toward the decisions you made as a child that are influencing your ideas about parenting, and one exercise to complete with your partner that will identify if your goals intersect, run parallel or diverge.

In Part II you and your partner will use the information from Part I to craft your own co-parenting plan. There are detailed instructions in Chapter 7. You can work your way through the book chapter by chapter or jump around. There is no right or wrong way to approach the work, and you might decide to start with the areas of life where you and your partner seem to work well together and tackle the areas where you struggle at a later time.

While each couple's challenges are different and unique, they all have one thing in common: each partner comes to parenting with ideas, attitudes, beliefs and perspectives based on their childhood experiences. All of these then became goals for the future and the path that each unique person anticipates taking to achieve the life he or she imagines for their families and themselves. As I have said, we don't know what we don't know, so providing specific questions, prompts and examples for couples to use as the framework for a new conversation about co-parenting successfully is the most logical place to begin.

First Things First

The work begins with you exploring your own childhood experiences. These general guidelines will help you stay the course, and when you deviate, will help you re-center and point you back toward your goal, to co-parent successfully for the sake of your kids, your marriage and your family. If you find that these guidelines are too rigid, forget about them, and if you find you need more, add them. These are guidelines, not absolutes. Remember, this is your process, and you and your partner are in a far better position to determine what will support this process to its most fruitful and rewarding end.

1. Be gentle with yourself. It will be easy to slip into a critical or judgmental frame of mind when you begin examining your childhood memories. There is no need. You do not have to defend yourself, justify yourself or explain yourself. You are here to learn about yourself, so try and maintain a learner's mind-set, and the exploration will be more enjoyable and fruitful.

2. If you find yourself struggling, take a break. Let your thoughts or memories or any images you may have per- colate in your mind and your heart for 24-hours and come back to them again at a different time or place.

3. Strong emotions are bound to arise and when they do, make space for them and rather than trying to under- stand them, let them be. Keep a journal handy to write down anything you might want to explore at a later time. When the emotions have settled, see if you can use them to uncover a story you may have been telling yourself that is more fiction than fact or allows you to see a situa- tion in a new light that is liberating rather than constrict- ing. Embrace whatever comes up and let it lead you to answers that are true and meaningful for you. This can be transformative work when we commit to staying put even as the fear tries to drive us away.

4. Think in terms of the "I," rather than the "we" format. Answer any questions and tell your stories using "I," not "we." "When I get angry, I. . ." (rather than when "we," or "when people"). Your job is to explore your own experi- ences. Watch how easy it is to make the statement "We all thought our parents were too strict," to include your sib- lings. This may or may not be accurate, but it is irrelevant for this exercise. You are talking only of yourself. Believe it or not, this is a tricky area, and many corporations, leader- ship development programs and self-help groups employ this technique as a way to keep communication clean. Watch how often you try to enlist others in your ideas. It's a defense mechanism meant to make us feel safe. It is your way of telling yourself, *I'm not alone in my thinking*. But this can creep into your parenting, and when this happens you group your children with you. You communicate to your partner, "See, the kids feel the same way about you as I do"! This may or may not be true, and even if it is true, it is not your place to bring the kids into your fight. Doing so can and often does cause irreparable damage to your mar- riage and to the relationship you have with your children.

5. Be as honest and as ruthless as you can when answer- ing questions or writing statements that capture your

experiences. This requires courage and commitment, but then so does raising kids, so I know you can do it. Tap into your inner resources and remind yourself that the more honest you are, the better your chances are of parenting with your partner and for your kids, with a sense of integrity, clarity and open-mindedness.

Memories Carry Meaning

In Chapters 4, 5 and 6, you will find questions, prompts, statements and mini stories to help you retrieve your childhood memories in specific areas of your life. This is the most important part of this work. Understanding yourself and how your past influences you today will bring a sense of clarity to your current parenting practices, and make it easier for you and your partner to work together going forward.

It is important that you begin your exploration on your own so you have time to reflect and to flush out all the hidden beliefs, attitudes, ideas and values you have developed. It is also a time to re-examine experiences and to find new insights where you least expect them. You may also identify patterns that either help or hinder the process of parenting and working cooperatively with your co-parenting partner.

Exercise One: Self-Discovery

Think of Exercise One as your opportunity to revisit your childhood and gather memories and impressions from childhood, identify how those past experiences are influencing your present day parenting practices, and a chance to capture any *aha moments* or insights you stumble upon as a result of this exploration into your past. To make it easier, I have broken out the three parts to this exercise. Eventually after some practice, you will be able to write a few sentences that include all three of these elements.

Impressions from Childhood

The prompts and mini stories are designed to stimulate impressions from your childhood. You can circle the statements that apply, write your own or just allow your childhood memories to come into clear focus and capture them in a few sentences. For example, "My parents had high expectations of their kids. I walked around wondering when I would be corrected for doing something wrong or for disappointing them in some way. It was like walking on eggshells. I was tense, uneasy and looked for any reason to get out of the house whenever I could." The important thing is to allow these memories to surface and to be as honest as you can when you write those memories down.

From Past to Present

When you have captured your memories, write down any decisions you made based on those memories. These decisions grew into a concrete belief system that is currently influencing every parenting decision you make. Yes, you did make decisions about how you would parent when you, yourself were being parented. For example, "I was raised on junk food and had twenty-two fillings before the age of twenty. I decided to feed my children healthy, sugar free, organically grown food to ensure their health."

Beliefs should not be taken lightly. They are at the center of every argument we find ourselves in. It is easy to run into trouble if one parent believes that responsible parents feed their children nothing but organically grown food and the other parent believes feeding them ice cream, if it creates fond memories of childhood, is what any loving and responsible parent would do. If both parents are willing to consider the other's beliefs, and let go of absolutes, there is an opportunity for these parents to redefine what responsible means, how much organic is enough, and when honoring a memory is more important than saying no to a bowl of ice cream. When we reframe our ideas, it opens up possibilities we didn't see before. I challenge any parent *not* to support a spouse who is re-creating a special childhood memory with their own child.

Insights Inspire Change

It is not unusual for parents to experience an *aha* moment or to gain some new insight and clarity after completing the first part of this exercise. Often, those *ahas* are about the dynamic with or between their co-parenting partner.

I know in my own life that when I experienced a powerful *aha* moment about myself, I was more willing to communicate openly and honestly with my partner because I felt less vulnerable and more powerful in this new awareness of myself. When this happened I could work with my partner to clear up any misunderstandings and concentrate on improving our relationship or a situation that until then had been causing undue stress and frustration for our children and ourselves. For example, when I become angry it is a secondary emotion to feeling hurt. I am less inclined to show my hurt because I feel weak and vulnerable. I feel more powerful and in control when I am angry because I am on the offensive. When I realized that I was choosing to be angry to cover feeling vulnerable, it was easier for me to acknowledge my emotion and articulate what was going on for me before there was a big blowup.

After finishing Exercise One, you might notice common themes or patterns in your thinking that inform your decision making and ultimately, the action or reactions you have to certain behaviors you see in your spouse and kids.

You will find examples from clients that I have worked with throughout the book to help illustrate for you how to connect these themes and patterns to your decision making and then your reactions and behaviors. The hope is that by reading how the process worked for someone else, it will be easier for you to apply it to your individual situation.

Exercise Two: Vision for the Future

After you have completed Exercise One, you will have a chance to write a vision for what you want in the future. It doesn't have to be elaborate or complicated. In fact, you might want to keep things exactly as they are, or make minor adjustments, and it's possible that you recognize a complete overhaul is in order because your goal for, say, a peaceful mealtime has been compromised, because you focused too much of your attention on teaching your kids good table manners. This is a chance for you to examine and perhaps challenge your priorities, and determine for yourself what is most important for you. Imagine how much easier it will be to work with your partner if you have already accepted that you may be too rigid or too lenient, too involved or not involved enough, in a particular area of your child's life, and you are willing to explore alternatives. Here is an example of where you are going.

Jeff and Susan

Both parents had very different ideas about bedtime. Because Jeff worked long hours, he coveted time with the kids in the evening. Susan agreed that it was important for Jeff to bond with the kids each evening and supported him when he asked to extend their bedtime by thirty minutes. Unfortunately for Susan, Jeff preferred to spend his time roughhousing rather than reading with the kids. This got the kids cranked up, and all of Susan's efforts to get them into bed at a reasonable hour were negated. After years of bedtime battles, making agreements neither of them followed, they used the exercises to flush out what kept them stuck in this toxic tango.

"We could have saved ourselves years of arguing had we done this exercise when we first noticed we were at odds when it came to bedtime," Pam recalled. As it turns out I have a story from my own childhood that includes a very chaotic home life that left me feeling uneasy, anxious and high strung. My only memories of feeling safe and settled were when my big brother read to me under the covers before I went to sleep. Jeff has a similar story that includes roughhousing with his dad, which was the only physical contact he ever had with him. It took minutes for us to appreciate our partners' experience (once we understood the other's perspective), and to agree to support both a bit of rough house and reading and then commit to creating our own bedtime ritual with our kids that included physical touch, along with a sense of safety and security for the kids. Now, each time Jeff tousles with the kids I smile instead of cringe, and he will gladly support all my attempts to nuzzle up with the kids and read."

Exercise Three: Intersect, Parallel, Diverge

When you and your partner revisit this section together, you will have an opportunity to share your childhood experiences from Exercise One and your goals for the future in Exercise Two. Remember, if you have the same goal, your parenting plan will help you set a clear course. When you get to this exercise, circle I if your goals intersect, P if they run parallel or D if they diverge. In Chapter 7 you will find a detailed explanation of what these identifying categories mean.

Janis and David

"I was raised in a very strict, religious household. I was not only influenced by my parents, but by their parents who spent a good deal of time at our home. I remember hearing the adults talk endlessly about good parents and bad parents, good kids and bad kids, and without knowing it I adopted many of their very judgmental beliefs about people. I worked on this in my adult relationships, but it didn't occur to me to explore how these concrete statements might affect my parenting. When I met David I was immediately attracted to his easy going, accepting nature and thought he would be a good influence on me. And he was until we had kids and then all hell broke loose. My beliefs about good and bad, right and wrong were so rigid that his 'no worries' attitude almost did me in. I wanted kids who displayed good manners from the time they were two; he trusted the kids would learn in time. I wanted our kids to show respect for all their elders; he figured if they didn't hit or spit at an adult that was good enough. The more I dug in my heels about the 'proper way' of raising kids, the more David resisted anything I had to say. He summarized me as being rigid, self-righteous and judgmental to a fault. I was so hurt that I started to pit the kids against him and I hated myself for it, but I just couldn't let go of those ingrained messages from my childhood. I was certain we would divorce. Thankfully, after working for a few months exploring our childhoods and really listening to how each of us created our beliefs about parenting, we began to see ways we could come together in the best interest of our kids. I won't say it was always easy, but it was always worth it. Today, we enjoy a much more relaxed approach to our parenting and when I dig in, we know exactly what to do to loosen those rigid thoughts. If we can do this work, anyone can do it. These exercises saved our marriage."

In order to execute your parenting plan successfully you will need to understand that you (the parents) have two different backgrounds, a set of varied beliefs and two very different ideas of the kind of parent you want to be. Even after taking all these variables into consideration, you must remember to communicate in a way that is empowering, encouraging, flexible and tolerant.

The only thing left to do is turn the page and get started. But before you do, pause here for a moment and imagine what life will be like for you and your parenting partner when you have established a foundation for co-parenting in an atmosphere of respect, support, acceptance and love. There is nothing you and your partner will not be able to handle together, and the feeling of cooperation and collaboration will be woven into every aspect of your life.

At the end of the day, it is not just our job; it is our responsibility to parent the children we have living with us. It is not to recreate, reject or reconstruct our own childhood experiences, but rather to make unified, thoughtful decisions necessary to raise emotionally healthy, self-reliant, cooperative and resilient people.

4

Family Relationships

It's time to explore your childhood relationships with family members and uncover memories that will help you better understand your current parenting practices. Each relationship within your family of origin is significant. The relationships with your primarily caregivers, whether that is mom and dad, two moms, two dads or any other combination, influence how you imagine yourself to be as a parent. The relationship you witnessed between your parents gives you hints as to the kind of co-parenting dynamic you want or don't want with your partner. Life with your siblings gives you clues as to how you will nurture the relationship between your own children in an effort to ensure they remain friends for life. Your early friendships will influence whether you encourage your children to develop large networks of friends or select only a few to round out their tribes.

Many, if not most, of the decisions you are currently making when it comes to your own family were made when you were young and impressionable. Those early impressions became generalizations you use to describe family relationships: *we were very close, I didn't get along with my siblings, my folks fought a lot, everyone was always pleasant to each other, we were really disorganized as a family,* or *my folks ran a tight ship.* We don't realize the powerful decisions we make on a daily basis, based on these seemingly unimportant generalizations. It's time for you to find out just how these relationships are influencing your own personal parenting practices and your ability to co-parent successfully with your partner.

In all likelihood the memory and decision will be in line with Dr. Walton's question (listed in Chapter 2): *I liked this or that about my family and want to do it the same way,* or *I found this unpleasant and do not want to do things this way.* In either case, capture these memories and think of them as treasures rather than an anchor aimed at dragging you back to your past.

Instructions

Complete Exercise One on your own. After reading through the prompts, recall your early childhood memories and impressions, the decisions you made based on those memories and any *aha* moments or insight as a result of your exploration.

Complete Exercise Two on your own. Write a vision for how you would like things to be going forward. It's possible you may want to make minor adjustments, or you understand that a complete overhaul is in order. You and your partner will share the vision for the future and determine if your ideas, views and perspectives intersect, run parallel or diverge.

Complete Exercise Three with your partner. After sharing your memories and your new vision for the future, decide with your partner if you think this is an area where your ideas, views and perspectives intersect, run parallel or diverge, so when you are ready to write a parenting plan together you can begin your work in the areas of life where you intersect.

The Relationship Between You and Your Parents

The relationship between you and each of your parents may be the most important relationship of your life. You made decisions about the roles of mothers and fathers based on your own childhood experiences with your parents, and those early decisions determine the kind of mother or father you hope to be and the kind of mother or father you want your partner to be for your children. If you were raised by a single parent, your parents were divorced and shared custody, or you were part of an extended family structure, you still made observations that will influence your ideas on relationships between parents and their children.

These statements are prompts to help stimulate memories from your childhood. Circle the ones that best capture your childhood experiences, or write your own.

Leadership

- My M/F did everything because I was either too slow or didn't do things correctly, or made a mess.
- My M/F wanted things done in a particular way, and I was told how to do them.
- My M/F was still doing things for me that I could do for myself, which made me feel incompetent.
- My M/F lectured me on being responsible.
- My M/F pointed out my mistakes in hopes I would stop making them.
- My M/F did not let me make many decisions for myself.
- My M/F had unrealistic expectations of me.
- My M/F waited on me so I could enjoy my childhood and do what I wanted.
- My M/F was wishy-washy when making decisions, and I felt like I had to figure things out myself.
- My M/F treated me like a valuable and contributing member of my family.
- My M/F took the time to teach me how to do things for myself.
- My M/F never overreacted when I made a mistake.
- My M/F gave me choices so I would learn how to take responsibility for myself and my actions.
- My M/F allowed me to make mistakes without making me feel worse.
- My M/F had reasonable expectations for me.

Communication

+ My M/F told me what to do and expected me to do it.
+ My M/F was often harsh and short.
+ My M/F yelled when I did something wrong or to get me to behave.
+ My M/F yelled but expected me to answer respectfully.
+ My M/F lectured, nagged, counted, and repeated things.
+ My M/F would not tolerate any backtalk from anyone.
+ My M/F sent mixed messages, and I had to figure out what they meant.
+ I couldn't trust that what my M/F said one minute would mean the same thing in an hour.
+ My M/F tried to explain, reason, and convince me to go along with a parenting decision instead of just telling me a decision had been made.
+ My M/F was sarcastic and condescending.
+ My M/F was very passive aggressive.
+ My M/F said "Good job" and "I am proud of you" constantly.
+ My M/F said what they meant, meant what they said and then followed through.
+ My M/F listened to me and was interested in what I said.
+ My M/F asked me questions to better understand my views and to help me figure things out.
+ My M/F was honest with me, and this built trust between us.
+ My M/F was open and forthcoming and was interested in hearing my ideas, thoughts and opinions.
+ My M/F talked with me rather than at me.
+ If my M/F lost their temper, they were comfortable apologizing and taking responsibility.

Connection

+ I could never please my M/F.
+ I knew my M/F loved me because they said they did, but they didn't show it in their actions.
+ My M/F wasn't that interested in my life as a kid.
+ My M/F pointed out the things that were wrong with me.

- The only time I felt really close to my M/F was when I excelled at something or accomplished high recognition.
- My M/F regularly asked me if I loved him/her and if I thought she/he was a good parent.
- My M/F made me the center of their universe.
- My M/F treated me more like a friend than a child who needed guidance.
- My M/F wanted to play and have fun with me more than he/she wanted to parent me.
- I felt loved and valued by my M/F.
- My M/F made time for me when I needed it.
- I felt close to my M/F throughout my childhood and teen years.
- I was able to talk about anything with my M/F.

Exercise One: Self-Discovery

Write a brief statement capturing your **impressions from childhood** between you and each one (include biological and step if applicable) of your parents. It may be helpful to think of three to five adjectives that describe them individually. Then identify any beliefs or decisions you made as a child that signify how your **past is influencing your present** and finish with any *aha* moments or new **insights**.

Here are a few examples from parents who completed the exercise.

Expectations Exclude Partner

Impressions from Childhood
"My mom was fair, reasonable, kind, loving, and supportive. My dad was a quiet force in the home, but I never really understood him or felt close to him."

From Past to Present
"I decided to emulate my mom's style of parenting and try and respond to my kids in the way I remember her responding to me. I know I want my partner to be an equal partner in our parenting and to take an active role in our children's lives. I want my kids

to be close to their dad and to know how much their dad loves and cares about them."

Insight
"I need to work on being more reasonable with my expectations of my kids. I think they are a bit over the top at times. Unknowingly, I have excluded my partner from certain areas of parenting, because I never saw my dad jump in or my mom encourage him to take a more active role with us kids. Unfortunately, I'm not sure I know how to go about making that happen."

Misplaced Favoritism

Impressions from Childhood
"When I was very young, I adored my father, who admitted that I was his 'favorite' child and lavished his love on me. Of course he did this same thing with all his kids. My mom was relegated to the organizer of our life, while my father got all our love and attention."

From Past to Present
"I decided I wanted to be the one our kids loved best, and I think I even expected that my partner would let me play this role and would take on the role of the 'grown-up' with our kids. I don't think it was a conscious decision, but when I consider my behavior, I have to admit that I am always jockeying to be the favorite."

Insight
"I can see how this has backfired in our family. The kids don't have a lot of respect for me and my partner ends up playing the bad cop, which is so unfair because he is a really reasonable guy. I want both of us to share these roles equally so our kids have a healthy model for the roles of mothers and fathers when they become parents."

Lacking Consistency
"I loved my folks and I always felt like the luckiest kid I knew. They were fun, kind, even-tempered and they loved me unconditionally. It's really hard to explain this to people. The atmosphere

at my home was peaceful. That is the only way to describe it. I truly believe that good parents who love their kids treat them like my parents treated me. What I am beginning to realize after giving my childhood memories serious thought is that my parents didn't really have to worry about money and so they weren't stressed about finances or having to work long hours. That had a huge impact on their attitudes about life, their ability to take things in stride, their availability to attend school and sports functions and talk with us when we needed them. As much as I wanted to be this kind of parent with my own kids, the truth is I am driven by my career. I feel guilty when I get preoccupied with work or miss some important event, and my parenting suffers as I jump from being too demanding to too lenient and ultimately give in. I provide no consistency at all. Of course, my partner, who is trying to keep up with me and my changing rules and strategies, is at a complete loss and is frustrated and annoyed with me. Can't blame him really."

Quality or Quantity

"My mom raised me and I know how hard it is to raise kids, work, and keep your own social life alive. I have so much respect for the way she lived her life and the way she treated me. She couldn't always go to my games or attend school functions, but I knew she was interested in me and did what she could when she could. I decided that if your kids know you love them and that you are doing your best, they will be happy. My partner feels that I do not demonstrate enough interest in our children's lives. He has completely different experiences that shaped his opinion."

Leading by Example

"My childhood was pretty miserable. My parents drank, fought, left us alone a lot, yelled and then blubbered their apologies and expected everything to be okay. I had to take care of myself, and my younger sister and I remember feeling bitter and lonely as kids. I believe good parents lead by example and should hold themselves accountable when they mess up, and if they do their jobs, I believe they will raise children who are respectful, responsible and hardworking. I do my best to be the kind of person my kids can be proud of, but I think I am so focused on my looking good to others and having people tell me what a great dad I am that I put too much pressure on the kids to look good, do good and be good. My partner has pointed this out to me on many occasions, and I deny her observations each time. I need to really talk with her about how I can be the kind of parent my kids need, how to be a better partner and stop worrying about what the outside world thinks of me."

Focused on Feedback

"My father focused on where I needed to improve and took every opportunity to point out my shortcomings. I don't remember ever receiving any positive feedback from him, and at some point I gave up any idea that he was proud of me or my accomplishments. I decided I would focus on my children's accomplishments and let them know how proud I was of them, so they felt good about themselves, and I would overlook their mistakes unless they were really serious. The result is that my kids need constant positive feedback and fall apart if I want to talk about a mistake or an area of life they need to improve in. My goal to raise kids with strong self-esteem who were also resilient backfired."

Exercise Two: A Vision for the Future

Using what you have discovered, write your vision for the future, including any action items you will incorporate into daily life with your family.

Here are some examples from clients to help illustrate this exercise.

Radical Faith

"My grandmother was my role model. She would tell it like it was and love you all up at the same time. Because I was secure in her love for me, I trusted her to guide me. She had radical faith in herself, in our family and in me. I want my children to look back on their lives as children and say the same thing about me— that no matter what was happening, I had radical faith in them and their abilities. I will give them space to make decisions and mistakes and trust that they will be able to handle the outcome.

This is a bit of a departure for me, as I can be a hovering parent at times."

Building on Trust

"I want the relationships in my family to be based on trust. I want my kids to know that they can trust me to do what I say and follow through. I want them to trust that no matter what happens or what mistake they make, they can trust that our relationship is not based on their achievements or behavior. I will have to incorporate language that indicates all of this, because right now, my message is getting lost in all the lecturing I do."

Exercise Three: Intersect, Parallel, Diverge

When you and your partner revisit this section, you will have a chance to share your experiences from Exercise One and Two and then move forward in creating a shared vision and a parenting plan to support that vision.

Based on your experiences, do you believe this is an area where you and your partner I (intersect), P (run parallel) or D (diverge)? Circle the best identifying category.

Parents as Parenting Partners

As children, we watch how our parents either work together in the best interest of their children or work against each other at the risk of their children. Sometimes it's a bit of both. If you were raised by a single parent, your parents were divorced and shared custody, or you were part of an extended family structure, you still made observations that will influence your ideas on co-parenting. Based on your observations it's fair to say that you made decisions about the best way to co-parent with your partner and what it meant to co-parent successfully. Of course, these decisions were made long before we knew how difficult parenting was, but we made those decisions nonetheless, and they are still influencing us today. It's time to think of your own parents as partners and consider what decisions you may have made.

Circle the statements that best represent your parents' co-parenting style, or write your own statement that captures their unique style.

My Parents' Overall Ideas on Raising Children
◆ Didn't align, and they were at odds with each other and fought often.
◆ Were consistent with each other, and they worked together to raise their kids.
◆ Were very different, and they went behind each other's back when dealing with kid issues.
◆ Varied on some topics and aligned on others, but they were great role models for how to co-parent successfully.
◆ Were never discussed; however they were always a united front and we knew we could never pit one against the other.

When My Parents Didn't Agree on an Issue
Concerning Their Children
◆ They criticized each other openly with a cutting intolerance.
◆ They respectfully considered the other's opinion and found common ground.
◆ One parent was always giving in to please the other.

My Parents Fought about How to Raise Their Children
◆ Often and openly, whether the kids were around or not.
◆ Frequently, but it never escalated to screaming.
◆ From time to time, but always in a calm and respectful manner.
◆ They disagreed, but it was over quickly.

When My Parents Communicated on the Topic of Parenting
◆ They listened, acknowledged, and respected the other person's ideas and opinions.
◆ They spoke over each other, needing to be right or have the final say.

- It was the bare minimum, just enough to keep the household operating.

I Often Felt
- Confused, frustrated, and anxious when I knew one of my parents was going against the other.
- Confident that both my parents were on the same page.
- Secure in the knowledge that my parents would work together in the best interest of their kids.
- I could play one parent against the other because they both had different ideas on parenting.
- Overwhelmed and wished they would just get divorced to end all the fighting.

When It Came to Co-parenting as a Team
- If one of my parents was too hard on us, the other parent would make up for it later.
- Even if one parent didn't agree with the other, they supported each other in front of the kids.
- I knew my parents talked over issues concerning their kids on a regular basis.
- My parents only worked together when there was a big issue; otherwise they deferred to the other.
- One of my parents would often override a decision the other parent made.
- I noticed tension between my parents when there was a serious situation with one of their kids.

Exercise One: Self-Discovery

Write a brief statement capturing your childhood experiences and memories surrounding co-parenting. As kids, we don't really consider the ramifications of our parents choosing to work against each other rather than with each other. As an adult and parent, you understand that this choice is the difference between a long and healthy marriage or the possibility of an early ejection, if you can't find a way to cooperate with your parenting partner.

Here are a few examples from parents who completed the exercise.

Quick to Compromise

Impressions from Childhood
"My parents made co-parenting look easy. They talked, shared ideas, included us in conversations and trusted that everything would work out eventually. I was a very relaxed kid who relished his childhood and wanted the same for my kids."

From Past to Present
"I believed that co-parenting with my partner would be as easy as my parents made it look. I wanted to co-parent and to make mutually agreed upon decisions about everything. I imagined long conversations that ended with us coming up with ideas, solutions and strategies to make our children's lives better."

Insight
"Wake up call here. My parents are introverts so they don't talk a lot in general and are quick to work toward an agreement rather than fight for their position. I am not my mother and my partner is not my dad, so we had to start from scratch. I am headstrong, laser-focused and once I make up my mind, it's hard to get me to change course. My partner is mellow and could be—no, is— easily manipulated into giving in to my demands. Oops. This is not what I want and I don't believe this models a healthy partner-ship for our kids."

Learning Communication Skills

Impressions from Childhood
"My dad had absolutely no say in how the kids were raised, and if he even suggested an idea or questioned my mother, she would come unhinged. After she was done screaming, she would play the victim and we would all end up apologizing and catering

to her tantrum. Then she would reward our giving into her by being absolutely delightful until the next time my dad opened his mouth."

From Past to Present
"I know I decided that I would never give up my parental authority. I think I wanted to work with my partner, but I'm not really sure I knew what that meant. I saw the bully and the victim play out, but never a cooperative relationship between my parents. I knew I never wanted my kids to witness what I did as a kid or feel like they were in the middle of our battles."

Insight
"Not only are my partner and I charged with the responsibility of identifying how we can co-parent; we also need to back up and make sure we learn and implement respectful communication skills, or we'll be headed down the same path as my parents."

Division of Labor
"I don't remember ever considering that my parents were required to co-parent. My mom was in charge of certain areas of our life and my dad other areas of my life. I knew who to go to when I had a question or who was going to punish me if I messed up. I loved this style of co-parenting and the clear division of labor and areas of authority, and truth be told, I wanted to design my own partnership just like this. I didn't understand why exactly until I finished this exercise. Here is the big *aha*; I didn't want anyone questioning my parenting decisions, and this was a good way to accomplish that goal. When you delegate certain areas to one parent or the other like my partner and I have, it means no one interferes with what I want. After all, I'm in charge. I disregard any of my partner's thoughts, ideas or observations and flatly state, 'Stay on your side of the court. That is the agreement.' First of all, he never really agreed to this, and second, I am bullying everyone in my family so I can do what I want."

Decision Making

"I was raised by a single mom and co-parenting meant either working things out with my dad over the phone, which she did with some success, or coming to a decision about something and then talking it over with me. I remember thinking that I wanted to have someone to bounce ideas off of so I didn't have to make them alone. My decision was clear: find someone I can trust and work with them to make every decision, so if things go wrong, it's not all on you. My poor partner. I use her like a crutch. I am so scared I will mess up that I make her talk about every little thing concerning the kids. She is exhausted, but I frame my desire for us to work together as a team so convincingly that she gives in. The truth is, I am afraid. If I want to create a more equitable relationship with my partner (which I do because otherwise she might eject me soon) and build up some courage so my kids see me as a confident parent, I need to start making decisions and stop worrying about the outcome."

Part of a Committee

"Step-families are tricky because you have multiple sets of parents who don't always see eye to eye. I think my parents, all of them, made on the spot decisions and hoped they wouldn't upset their partner or ex. It felt very confusing and I often wondered why they didn't have some sort of plan for how they were going to raise us. I know I made the decision in the eighth grade when none of my folks could agree on whether to let me attend a weekend function that was really important to me, that I would be the parent who made the hard choices if necessary and wouldn't leave it up to a committee of people who all had different ideas. For the most part, this approach has worked for the family, but I know I can bully my partner into doing what I want instead of opening up and considering her perspective. She asks really great questions, and I can dismiss them if it means I might change my mind after I have made a decision."

Strong Partnership

"Being raised by a single mom means watching her make every decision on her own and either feel good about it or question every parenting decision she made. My mom would bounce ideas off of her friends, read books on how to raise kids and even ask me what I thought about a decision she needed to make. I think I came away with the idea that there is no right or wrong way to raise kids, but that an open mind and a willingness to learn are more important than anything else. I think I am interested in what my partner thinks, and I am willing to give his way a try if I think it's in the best interest of the kids. All in all, our partnership is really strong, and I value his ideas, insights, perspectives and feedback."

Courage to Change

"I watched my dad bully my mom into submission without ever having to raise his voice. He did it with pious patronizing politeness. My mom would make a parenting decision, and for no reason at all, he would start to question why she wanted to do it that way and didn't she think it would be better if she did it another way. Before long, she would give in and do what he wanted. I swore that I would never back down or submit once I had made a parenting decision I thought was in the best interest of my kids. I jumped from one extreme to the other without knowing it. When my partner is correct in challenging a decision I make, I cut him off at the knees. I am no better than my dad. This new insight gave me the courage to deal with my resistance to 'giving in' out of fear of being bullied, and work hard at reframing my ideas of what it means to co-parent. My new motto is *clarity gives me the courage to change*."

Exercise Two: A Vision for the Future

Using what you have discovered, write your vision for the future, including any action items you will incorporate into daily life with your family.

Here are some examples from clients to help illustrate this exercise.

Finding Middle Ground

"I don't want our family to have a strict parent and an easy going parent, which is how it would be if my partner and I just parented from our natural tendencies. It is important for both of us to move to the middle on almost every topic, as our childhood experiences and the decisions we made were extremely different when it came to raising kids. I can't believe we never discussed it until it caused problems. I just assumed. So as we go through and create our plan, we both know that my instinct would be too soft and her instinct too harsh and we'll move to a middle ground."

Addressing Differences

"Since I stay at home and spend most of the time with the children, my partner wants me to make the decisions and just move forward. He says he'll support whatever decision I make. This feels a bit like a setup, so we'll start with the areas we diverge and address those right away; then the areas we intersect or parallel can be addressed later."

Exercise Three: Intersect, Parallel, Diverge

When you and your partner revisit this section, you will have a chance to share your experiences and move forward in creating a shared vision and a parenting plan to support that vision.

Based on your experiences do you believe this is an area where you and your partner I (intersect), P (run parallel) or D (diverge)? Circle the best identifying category.

The Relationship Between You and Your Siblings

How many of us look at our own children and wonder what we can do to ensure they stay friends for life? Isn't that desire based on our own experiences with our siblings? Whether you look forward to seeing your siblings during holiday visits or it causes you a severe case of anxiety, the relationships you had with your siblings while you were living at home together shape your views, ideas and beliefs regarding sibling relationships.

Circle the statements that best represent your childhood memories, or write your own statements to capture life at home with siblings as you were growing up.

Teasing, Fighting and Other Forms of Conflict

+ My parents let us fight and work things out on our own.
+ My parents intervened in all our arguments.
+ Someone was always punished if there was a fight between the kids.
+ My parents weren't interested in hearing what the fight was about, just that it stopped.
+ I don't remember getting into trouble if we fought.
+ My siblings and I fought all the time.
+ I think I fought with my siblings but not enough to remember.
+ I teased my brother/sister mercilessly.
+ I was teased by my brother/sister every day.

Bonds

+ I was close to all my siblings.
+ My siblings and I enjoyed playing together.
+ I got along with one or two of my siblings.
+ I didn't get along with any of my siblings.
+ My siblings were okay, but I didn't have much to do with them.
+ I consider my siblings my best friends.
+ I didn't trust my siblings.
+ I adored my brother/sister.
+ We were forced to spend time with each other.
+ The only time we got along was when we were busy doing something.

Pecking Order

+ I was the leader of the pack.
+ My brother/sister was leader of the pack.
+ My brother/sister excluded me.
+ I excluded by brother/sister.
+ I told on my brother/sister so I would be the favorite.
+ My brother/sister told on me so I would get into trouble.
+ My parents favored one sibling over another.

Exercise One: Self-Discovery

Write a brief statement capturing your childhood experiences surrounding life with siblings, and any beliefs or decisions you made, and finish with *aha* moments or new insights.

Here are a few examples from parents who completed the exercise.

Demanding Attention

Impressions from Childhood
"This is going to sound awful, but I couldn't stand my brother growing up. He was needy, demanding and always getting into trouble. He monopolized my parents' attention, and I resented him from the time I was very young."

From Past to Present
"I swore that I would give my kids the same attention, and if I had a child who tried to monopolize my attention, I would ignore them. This exercise was really painful for me."

Insight
"I realize that my own child, who struggles with social skills and is a true introvert, needs extra attention, not because he is naughty or needy, but because he is slower at processing what is going on around him and mustering up the courage to participate in life. Instead of supporting and encouraging him, I have sent the messages that he isn't worth my time. My partner and I have been arguing fiercely about this for years, and he has been right the entire time. I owe everyone an apology."

Strong Sibling Bonds

Impressions from Childhood
"My siblings and I got along just fine. We all had our own friends, hobbies, and sports, so the time we spent together at home was pretty easy. There wasn't much fighting between us, but we weren't all that close either."

From Past to Present
"I decided that I wanted my children to develop strong bonds and share interests that would keep them connected as they grew older."

Insight
"I am so worried about my children being friends that I overreact and get in the middle of all of their fights. I make things worse, not better. I know stepping back is the smart thing to do, but I don't know how to do that in a balanced sort of way. It occurs to me that I could be helping them learn how healthy relationships work, so that they decide they want that with their siblings."

Competition or Cooperation
"My sister and I were best friends from the get go. I was still snuggling in bed with her when I was a teenager. When I was young, I dreamed that my own kids would have the same kind of relationship with their siblings. I really believed that this type of bond was possible between siblings and would happen naturally, and if they weren't close, then it must be my fault. I imagined the loss they would feel if they missed out on this kind of bond with a sibling, and I couldn't let that happen. This exercise opened my eyes to reality. My two children are polar opposites in terms of interests and personalities. They are in constant competition with each other and make every effort to be right or be the best, or even get the last word in during an argument. I can't force my kids, but I can start helping them see that they could turn their competitive relationship into one that benefited both of them."

Prepared for Disappointment
"I was part of a blended family, and I remember the day my younger brother went from being my best buddy to being best friends with our stepbrother. I felt betrayed and bitter. I have brought this resentment into my present day relationships, and I don't trust that most people won't turn on you if someone better shows up. I realize I project this onto each one of my kids and my partner. I am preparing all of us for disappointment instead of modeling trust, connecting and love."

Friend Instead of Parent

"My siblings and I were bounced from one house to the next after a bitter divorce. We had to stick together or be torn apart. We developed loyalties to each other rather than to our parents. I consider my siblings my family, not my parents. When my children came along, I vowed we would not have that type of us versus them family atmosphere. In an effort to keep us connected, I have become my children's friend more than parent. This drives my partner crazy, as my children do not respect or value my authority. My partner is a natural leader and has qualities that I admire and respect. I have never had the courage to ask him to help me in this area of life, but if I want to stay married and I want what is best for my kids, then it's time to put my ego aside and learn from my partner."

Meddling Moderator

"My parents thought their kids should 'work things out' on their own. All I know is that I got pounded by my older brother and I knew I would never let that happen with my kids. I was going to make sure that they would not use physical violence to work out their problems and that meant that I would be intervening each time there was a squabble. The result is that my kids tattle on each other a dozen times a day and have no idea how to work out even the simplest disagreement without me there to help. And, unknowingly, I have pitted them against each other by punishing whoever gets tattled on. My partner is fed up with the fact that I am always in the middle of the kids' fight, and then we start fighting about that. I think I'm ready to revamp this area of life, and I think my partner is going to have a whole lot of ideas on where to start."

Normal Sibling Rivalry

"I am an only child and I have no frame of reference on how siblings interact, how much sibling rivalry is normal or when kids should stop taking showers together. It's all new to me, and I lose my confidence quickly when it's time to make a decision that I have no prior experience in. To cover my insecurity I make quick decisions that oftentimes confuse situations or make things worse. I can't tell you how many times I have looked at my partner to catch her shaking her head in disbelief. It means a lengthy evening conversation while I try and justify myself. I think I can see that coming to an end with this new clarity and my willingness to explore options."

Natural Problem Solving

"My siblings and I were very close as kids. We did everything together and figured out the pecking order and how to solve our disagreements. There wasn't much physical fighting or name calling. I think we must have established some code of conduct we all lived by. I decided to give my kids lots of room to work out their relationships with a minimal amount of interference with me. The result so far is that the kids are remarkably close and can solve most of their problems without much help from me. Having a partner who trusted me in the beginning when the kids were figuring things out went a long way in our success in this area of life."

Exercise Two: A Vision for the Future

Using what you have discovered, write your vision for the future, including any action items you will incorporate into daily life with your family.

Here are some examples from clients to help illustrate this exercise.

Opportunity to Practice

"I will stop worrying about the future and focus on supporting my children as they learn effective and respectful communication and problem solving skills. This means letting go of any prior expectations and beliefs and provide my children with an opportunity to practice."

Support My Relationships

"My children's relationships with each other are between them. I will focus my energy on my relationship with my spouse and my children and trust that the bonds we create will develop as they should. There isn't anything I can do to predict the future. Worrying about it may foster what I fear the most."

Exercise Three: Intersect, Parallel, Diverge

When you and your partner revisit this section, you will have a chance to share your experiences and move forward in creating a shared vision and a parenting plan to support that vision.

Based on your experiences, do you believe this is an area where you and your partner I (intersect), P (run parallel) or D (diverge)? Circle the best identifying category.

Friendships

Growing up, each of us experienced both positive and negative encounters when it came to our friendships. Some relationships were deep and meaningful, and we associate joy and connection with each memory and person. Others were the breeding ground for betrayal and rejection, and we as parents don't want our children to experience the isolation and pain that we ascribe to our childhood friendships. These experiences fuel the decisions we make about our children, their friendships and how we will support them as they learn to navigate this sometimes tricky area of their lives. It's easy to miss how an event from so far back in our past is guiding the decisions we are making for and around our children, but they are.

Circle the statements that best capture your childhood experiences.

- ◆ My parents wanted me to have a huge social network.
- ◆ My parents were always scheduling "playdates" for me with appropriate friends.
- ◆ We had a big family, and my parents preferred I spend time with my siblings.
- ◆ I attended a private school 45 minutes from our home. I was never allowed to travel to spend time with my schoolmates.

- If I wasn't invited to a birthday party or celebration, my mother would call and have me invited.
- My parents were always meddling in my friendships and calling my friends' parents.
- My parents worried that I only had two friends. I think for them it was quantity over quality.
- My parents could not tolerate my best friend. It was very difficult for us to spend time together.
- My parents trusted that I was able to judge character and that I would make mistakes and be able to navigate the outcomes of my choices.
- I think my parents wanted to be my best friend.
- My parents were my confidantes and biggest champions. I was always closer to my parents than anyone else.
- My parents were threatened by my friendships with others.
- My parents were always supportive of my friends and social network.

Exercise One: Self-Discovery

Write a brief statement capturing your childhood experiences surrounding friendships. Then capture a belief or decision you made and finish with any *aha* moments or new insights.

Here are a few examples from parents who completed the exercise.

Reframing My Experience

Impressions from Childhood

"We moved when I was in the fifth grade, and I went from having neighborhood friends that felt like family to no friends at all which continued through high school. I always wanted friends, but I was awkward and felt the outsider so kept to myself. Writing this, I can see how that experience has influenced my ideas about friendships."

From Past to Present
"I wanted to save my kids from the heartache I felt, so I down-play the value of outside friendships in an attempt to shield them from experiencing the pain I felt. As a result, I am overly involved in their friendships and I begin to undermine them before they have had a chance to blossom."

Insight
"I have no faith in my children's ability to bounce back from a friendship that ends, and I am denying them a chance to develop deep and lasting friendships because of my own fear. Perhaps it's time for me to get some adult friends and let go of this old childhood story."

Neighborhood Bliss
"I was raised in a family neighborhood with kids my age all around. My parents would send me out of the house after school, and I would play with kids of every age until we heard our names called for dinner. I relish those memories and hope my kids have as many friends growing up as I did. I decided we would be the 'Kool-Aid' house. I wanted our home to be where all the neighborhood kids came to spend time. We even bought our dream house on a cul-de-sac, so I could set it up. My children are introverts and would so much rather be by themselves or with one close friend. I pushed and pushed them to live into my dream for them, but now it is time for me to let go and accept them for who they are. My partner is an introvert as well, and I think every time my children and I get in a fight about this, she thinks I am personally insulting her."

Forced Friendships
"I was a pretty shy kid and my parents were forever trying to force me to do things with other kids. The modern term is play-dates. I still cringe when I hear the word. It wasn't even so much that I was forced to play with other kids, but that my parents so blatantly disregarded what I wanted that influenced my decisions regarding my own kids and their friendships. I try to be very mindful about what my kids are thinking and feeling. My youngest child is very cautious. In an attempt to respect her

feelings, I have coddled her and not challenged her to take rea-sonable risks. My husband thinks we should push her out of her comfort zone, and I have not supported this effort. I see now that I am holding her back in an effort to be the parent that I wished my parents were for me. I understand that I am not parenting me, and what I would have preferred is not in her best interest."

Family Gatherings

"We had a big family with many cousins close by so I considered my family as my friends. I had friends in school, but anything I did outside of school I did with my siblings or cousins. We all moved away as we hit the college years, and I miss them. Almost every happy memory I have includes my siblings and my cous-ins. I want to give my kids the same kind of experience I had, so I built a big house and host all of my relatives three times a year for a weekend visit. These weekend visits put a strain on our family, and this exercise helped me to see why I am so motivated for these gatherings. I never stopped to consider that everyone wasn't as interested in this experience as I was. I just assumed it was how everyone looked at life."

Heartache and Rejection

"I suffered rejection and exclusion from my group of friends dur-ing middle and high school. 'Protect your children so they do not get hurt by mean children' became my motto. I realized that I was trying to protect my kids from the same heartache by downplay-ing the importance of their friendships. They stopped talking to me about their friends and began talking to my partner, and that infuriated me, so I lashed out at everyone. I didn't really under-stand how much that rejection in high school has influenced all my decisions surrounding friendships."

Popularity a Priority

"I wasn't a very popular kid, and so when my daughter came home in kindergarten upset that she wasn't invited to a birth-day party, all my fears were triggered and I called the mother to implore her to invite my daughter. Over the years, I have made my daughter's popularity a priority, and it has caused her and the family a number of problems. My partner has a more logical and realistic view, and it wasn't until I completed these exercises that I could see what I was doing."

Forever Friends
"I love my friends. I love the connection, the camaraderie and the fun. I push my kids to reach far and wide in search of the forever group of friends. None of them are as social as I was. Two of them don't even enjoy team sports. This push from me causes pushback from them. My wife would always try to convince me to back off, but I couldn't; I didn't want them to feel left out. Just reading the other statements offered clarity that not everyone navigates the world in the same way. Maybe it was just that I wasn't feeling criticized while reading these lists, and it left my mind open to consider another point of view."

Exercise Two: A Vision for the Future

Using what you have discovered, write your vision for the future, including any action items you will incorporate into daily life with your family.

Here are some examples from clients to help illustrate this exercise.

Developing Self-Worth
"I want to help my children understand that they are not defined by birthday parties, sleepovers, likes on their social media pages, sports teams or the number of friends they have. I am not sure right at this moment how I will pull this off, but I think a good place to start would be to get more information on building self-worth in kids, and how to help them bounce back from life's disappointments."

Opportunities to Connect
"I am my own best friend and truthfully enjoy my own company more than anyone else's, but I realize the ability to connect with others is valuable, so I will support my children to make connections outside of the family."

Exercise Three: Intersect, Parallel, Diverge

When you and your partner revisit this section, you will have a chance to share your experiences and move forward in creating a shared vision and a parenting plan to support that vision.

Based on your experiences, do you believe this is an area where you and your partner I (intersect), P (run parallel) or D (diverge)? Circle the best identifying category.

Adjusting the Focus

The stories in this chapter reflect very different experiences. Relationships, especially those with family members, can be confusing, exhilarating, loving, distant, mysterious and mercurial. By now, perhaps they are coming into sharper view, and you can begin to see the impact they have on your current parenting practices and your ability to co-parent successfully with your partner.

You will return to this chapter with your spouse and use Exercise Three to determine whether your experiences, beliefs and vision for the future intersect, run parallel or diverge, and then begin to construct a thoughtful parenting plan that will guide your decision-making process for years to come. Until then, let's move on to another area of family life and explore the day-to-day living in a family.

5

Daily Operations

You have arrived here, after completing a set of exercises focused on your family relationships and friendships. No doubt revisiting your childhood brought up a barrage of impressions, memories and feelings. The entire process could have been quite emotional, however extremely important. All of the information you gathered is going to make it possible for you and your partner to come together in a deep and meaningful way and begin to co-parent with love, acceptance, respect and intention.

Exploring every aspect of day-to-day life would be impossible, so I have highlighted those areas that after twenty-five years of working with parents I have identified as causing the most confusion and dissension when it comes to co-parenting successfully. I have also included at the end of the chapter a list of additional topics for you to explore if you believe there is something for you to learn about yourself and your current parenting practices in those other areas of daily life.

The Money Dance
"Sarah and I dated for five years before we decided to take the plunge. Exploring the day-to-day operations of life exposed an

area where our views on kids and money diverge significantly. The general conversation went something like this:

Me: I want the kids to have money so they develop a deep appreciation for how slowly it comes and how quickly it goes.

Sarah: Yes and to develop a strong work ethic as well.

There you go. We both want the same things. Here is exactly where things went off the rails. I wanted our kids to have access to money and to learn about it through trial and error. Sarah wanted any money the kids got to be attached to their good grades and helping out with chores without making a fuss. Our differences were clearly exposed, and we were able to talk about where these ideas came from and how we could reframe them and develop new strategies to support our kids as they fostered a relationship with money. We recognized that without this clarity, it is likely that we would have fought for our positions, rather than considering what would be best for our kids. And given our personalities, we knew that once we started down a combative road, we would do whatever we could to convince the other to see things our way—a cycle that would have cost us all dearly."

Part I Instructions

Note: You will find these instructions below are the same as Chapter 4 and will be the same in Chapter 6. This work can be difficult, and if you've heard of or know me, you know I like to keep it simple. Life is complicated enough, and exploring your childhood is damn hard work—that's why in my book, the instructions will be easy to grasp.

Complete Exercise One on your own. After reading through the prompts, recall your early childhood memories and impressions, the decisions you made based on those memories and any *aha* moments or insight as a result of your exploration.

Complete Exercise Two on your own. Write a vision for how you would like things to be going forward. It's possible you may want to make minor adjustments or you understand that a complete overhaul is in order. You and your partner will share the vision for the future and determine if your ideas, views and perspectives intersect, run parallel or diverge.

Complete Exercise Three with your partner. After sharing your memories and your new vision for the future, decide with your partner if you think this is an area where your ideas, views and perspectives, intersect, run parallel or diverge, so when you are ready to write a parenting plan together, you can begin your work in the areas of life where you intersect.

Dinner

Evening meals were a time for the family to reconnect, share stories of their day and prepare for the evening together, or they were rushed and tense, where conflict could erupt at any minute if someone was in a bad mood, didn't like the meal that was offered or a squabble started between siblings. In my experience, most parents want the same thing—to create a Normal Rockwell dinner experience. One in which everyone is kind, polite, uses their manners, enjoys the meal, engages in pleasant conversation and then helps clear the table so that everyone can retire to the family room to play a board game.

Prompt

Think back to when you were a young child, perhaps between five or six years old, perhaps older, and put yourself at the dinner table. Look around and in your mind describe what is happening. Where were you sitting and who were you sitting next to? Did you always sit in the same place? What happened if someone wanted to change seats? Were your parents at the table with you? What feeling did you have as you sat there with your family? When you have a clear picture, decide if this represents the majority of your memories surrounding dinner with your family. You will notice certain themes, patterns, attitudes or perhaps even rituals that best capture this experience.

Exercise One: Self-Discovery

Write a brief statement capturing your childhood experiences surrounding dinnertime, any beliefs or decisions you made and finish with *aha* moments or new insights.

Here are a few examples from parents who completed the exercise.

Mealtime Guilt

Impressions from Childhood
"I remember mealtime feeling like a happy gathering of the family. There was always conversation that included the kids but we were also expected to listen and to learn. We were asked to sit just a few minutes longer than we thought we could and then were excused where we could go and play. When it was time to clean up, we were called back and were expected to help the adults."

From Past to Present
"I loved dinner with my family and I wanted my kids to have this same experience. I had in my mind that I would prepare these great meals that everyone would love and we would all talk and laugh and eat and my kids would love dinnertime as much as I had when I was a child."

Insight
"I am a busy working mom with four kids, and making the kinds of meals my mom put together is out of the question. I am so harried at the end of the day that making dinner increases my stress level, and by the time I call the kids to the table, I am in no mood to do anything other than eat, clean up and get them ready for bed. I feel guilty that I am not re-creating my own childhood memories for my kids, and that guilt comes out as a short temper and irritable attitude. My partner asks what she can do and I bark at her rather than explaining how let down I feel and asking for help."

Mealtime Memories

Impressions from Childhood
"My parents were so busy that mealtime was a time to eat what was put in front of you, instead of a time to visit and reconnect as a family. It wasn't unusual for my parents to multitask through most meals. I felt like I was eating alone most of the time."

From Past to Present
"I didn't want this kind of memory for my own kids. I know how important sharing dinner is and I was committed to making dinner a time for our family to connect and share their day. And I had a belief that 'good' children would also care about having dinner as a family and would contribute to the success of the meal."

Insight
"I never once talked with my partner or my kids about what they wanted dinner to look like and how we could create that together. We have a very unique family dynamic, and I took it upon myself to design a plan and try and execute it all on my own. My family is bewildered when I roll my eyes, or sigh at the table when things aren't the way I had planned and expect."

Nagging Questions
"Mealtimes meant stress to me, as they were always the time to hear about how you had to do better, stop doing something, or answer questions that were bound to start a fight. I ate as fast as I could, asked to be excused and found something else to do. I made the decision not to do what my parents did to me to my kids. But of course, that is exactly what I do, except I dress it up with a nice voice, probing questions and constructive feedback, but the effect is the same. The kids are resistant to eating together as a family, quiet and sullen when they come to the table and I end up feeling like an old nag by the time we finish. So, I guess the question I need to answer is, what am I going to do to ensure my kids have great memories of family dinners?"

Tension and Torture

"Family dinners were awful. My parents hardly spoke to each other and they brought all that anger and tension to the table where we were supposed to magically have this wonderful family meal. I swore I would never put my kids through the kinds of mealtimes I was forced to sit through, but instead of finding a balance, I have swung too far the other way. It is bedlam during every meal. Kids getting up and down, fussing about food, wanting me to cook something else, fighting with each other about where to sit, and then I jump in the fray and try and calm everyone down. My partner just sits and shakes his head in disbelief. All he wants is a quiet, somewhat peaceful mealtime, and I have created anything but that."

Rigid Expectations

"We were a family on the go and most mealtimes were a matter of grabbing something and eating in the car or standing at the counter. Now when I try and schedule family meals with my own kids, I think I am too rigid in what I expect from them. My partner has accused me of having unrealistic expectations of kids, and until now I thought he was just being critical, but I can see he has a point."

Note: When you finish with dinner, take a moment and do the same exercise around breakfast. It's possible your first meal of the day was a rushed experience as people tried to get out of the door on time, or a relaxed experience that set the tone for the rest of the day. What was it for you? How did it impact your beliefs about mealtime with your family?

Exercise Two: A Vision for the Future

Using what you have discovered, write your vision for the future, including any action items you will incorporate into daily life with your family.

Here are some examples from clients to help illustrate this exercise.

Reframing My Perspective

"Calm, connected, relaxed dinners are what I want. I tend to be an all or nothing person, and if it's less than a perfect dinner experience, I focus on what I am doing wrong. This discouragement gets transferred to the kids, and I start blaming them for a less than perfect meal. Knowing that this is an unrealistic expectation with four kids and two busy parents is the first step in me accepting that if we have two or three meals a week that resemble my vision, I am doing okay. I heard from other couples that their partner would help them reframe their perspective with nonverbal cues, and I think that might work for me now that I accept that things need to change."

Collaborative Effort

"I would like everyone to be involved in the mealtime experience from planning, to preparing, to serving, to cleaning up. This means that I need to let go of how things go and invite more participation and provide training. I am excited to move toward a collaborative effort, instead of feeling resentful by the end of the night."

Exercise Three: Intersect, Parallel, Diverge

When you and your partner revisit this section, you will have a chance to share your experiences from Exercises One and Two and then move forward in creating a shared vision and a parenting plan to support that vision.

Based on your experiences, do you believe this is an area where you and your partner I (intersect), P (run parallel) or D (diverge)? Circle the best identifying category.

Manners

Whether you were forced to practice good manners or you were raised in a relaxed home where manners weren't enforced but learned through watching your parents, most folks agree that manners make social gatherings more pleasant and relaxing for everyone concerned. Depending upon what culture you are raised in, the actions and responses that constitute good manners can vary. Regardless, we all as parents have beliefs about what manners mean to us, what kind we want our kids to embody, and how we are going to make sure we don't raise rude, ungrateful trolls.

Prompt

Imagine yourself as a school aged child and recall whether or not you heard your parents prompt you into saying please and thank you. Did they remind you to say hello or to look at someone when you are talking to them? Perhaps they coaxed you into apologizing if you made a mistake or hurt someone's feelings. Did they bring your attention to the use of forks, knives, napkins and asking for food to be passed rather than reaching across the table? How did your parents deal with burping, farting or other bodily functions? Watch yourself mature from a young child, to an elementary age person to a teen. Now fast forward until you were a teen. What has changed, if anything?

Exercise One: Self-Discovery

Write a brief statement capturing your childhood experiences surrounding manners. Then capture a belief or decision you made and finish with any *aha* moments or new insights.

Here are a few examples from parents who completed the exercise.

Prompts Invite Power Struggles

Impressions from Childhood

"My parents prompted me continuously about manners, politeness, saying please and thank you, and it made me feel like they had no faith in me whatsoever. It was embarrassing at times."

From Past to Present

"I was not going to put my kids through this humiliation. I decided that if I incorporated manners into daily life and modeled this for my children, they would grow into people who embodied manners."

Insight

"I struggle in situations where manners are expected and people have a different belief about teaching kids manner than I do. Most of the people I know think it is a parent's job to remind their kids or the kids won't learn. In these instances I panic and start to remind them. It never goes well. I feel like these reminders create power struggles and make the situation worse."

Modeling Manners

"My parents modeled the manners they wanted from their kids, and I think I picked up on that pretty early. People commented that I was polite, but I never really gave it any thought. It's just what you did. I definitely like this approach to teaching manners and use it with my children. I think for the most part, my partner and I would agree that this strategy is working, and it might be a model for us to use in other areas of our parenting life, where we can find ourselves arguing when it would be more beneficial to all of us to find a solution that works for all of us."

Plan for Politeness

"We were a very relaxed family, and our manners were not a big concern. I loved this until I got older and realized that I was kind of clueless. There has to be a balance between teaching your kids manners without making it feel like you are attending a class at the Emily Post Institute. I realize that I had no idea what to do, but that I am a bit embarrassed when my children act like cavemen when we are out in public. I think I need a plan."

First Impressions

"Manners equal good breeding and good first impressions. We were raised to believe you don't get a second chance to make a good first impression. Good manners were the most important value in our home, and I felt as though I couldn't speak my mind or even stand up for myself without being viewed as rude. This didn't feel right, and I wanted to create a balance for my children. In an effort to raise confident children who use their voices, I swayed far over to the other side and forgot about teaching my kids how to be polite. They speak to everyone like we speak to each other at home, raw and off the cuff. It is time I find a balance and use some methods to incorporate this feature into daily life. I think my partner will push back against this, but it is time. I am done feeling this way."

Surprising Results

"Manners are important to me, and I started teaching them to my kids when they were very young and continue to coach them at every opportunity. I don't want anyone to ever accuse my kids of being rude. I am surprised that my children still depend on me to prompt them and that good manners aren't more ingrained in them."

Opposing Perspectives

"Yes, manners are important when you are out in the world, but at home kids shouldn't be worried about that stuff. A family should be able to let loose at home. They will figure out they can't be rude or impolite when they are at their friend's homes. My partner doesn't agree."

Exercise Two: A Vision for the Future

Using what you have discovered, write your vision for the future, including any action items you will incorporate into daily life with your family.

Here are some examples from clients to help illustrate this exercise.

Develop Self-Confidence

"My daughter checks with me at every turn. Completing this exercise helped me to see that in an effort to raise a polite child, she won't speak without checking in with me first. Over the next year, I will focus on supporting my daughter to develop the confidence required to make decisions and speak for herself. This will require a change in so many areas, it just happened that manners is the area that opened up my understanding of how much I have been directing my daughter's life."

Relaxed Not Rude

"We are a crazy bunch of hooligans and I love it. Manners are overrated. I want my kids to have fun and feel free to be themselves. Anyone who closes doors or judges them for being raucous isn't going to be part of our lives for very long anyway. My partner doesn't agree, but I feel very strongly that I want life to be relaxed, real and fun."

Exercise Three: Intersect, Parallel, Diverge

When you and your partner revisit this section, you will have a chance to share your experiences and move forward in creating a shared vision and a parenting plan to support that vision.

Based on your experiences do you believe this is an area where you and your partner I (intersect), P (run parallel) or D (diverge)? Circle the best identifying category.

Toilet-Training

Once upon a time, kids were in charge of letting their parents know when they were ready to leave the diapers or nappies behind and begin using the toilet like their parents and older siblings. Not so anymore. There are gimmicks and games, toys and treats and even candy rewards all in an attempt to manipulate kids into toilet-training in order to make either our lives easier or to brag to our friends about how brilliant our little Suzie or Johnny is now at twelve-months-old and successfully using the big potty. Mind you, these poor tikes are probably getting prompted every minute or so. *Do you have to use the potty? Are you sure? Let's go try and use the potty?* When they refuse to perform on cue and finally do listen to their bodies and release, they usually find themselves on the other end of a lecture or a scolding from a parent who is tired of wiping up the pee or changing another outfit. All of this could be avoided if we listened to the experts and to our kids, but alas, in today's world, trying to force kids into one more behavior that makes our lives easier seems to be the norm.

Prompt

It might be hard to recall how your parents handled toilet-training, but somewhere deep in your memory you have stored information on whether you found this area of life stressful and possibly still have a few unresolved issues. Or you might talk to your parents about your experience and wait to see if you experience an *aha* moment as they discuss toilet-training. And it could be that you have no recollection at all, but at some point, you made a decision about toilet-training and your child. Take a few moments and either reflect on your childhood or see if you can pinpoint when you started considering how you would handle toilet-training with your child. Was it a conversation you had with friends who bragged about their child's potty-success, a book or blog you read, or are you trying to feel adequate as a parent and this is one way for you to gauge your progress and performance?

Exercise One: Self-Discovery

Write a brief statement capturing your childhood experiences and memories surrounding this area of life. Then capture a belief or decision you made and finish with any *aha* moments or new insights.

Here are a few examples from parents who completed the exercise.

Pressure to Perform

Impressions from Childhood

"I have no memories of potty-training, but my parents tell me that I was potty-trained by nine-months of age, and that I would crawl over to the toilet and climb up and ask for help. My mother still brags about how quickly I was potty-trained and I am still embarrassed when she does."

From Past to Present

"I promised myself I would not pressure my kids to use the toilet, just so I could brag about them, but when my son was born, I fully expected him to follow in my footsteps and when he didn't have any interest I started pressuring him. When he didn't perform, I took it personally and got frustrated with him."

Insight
"I created a power struggle over something that does not matter in the least. I am sad to say that he was still wearing a diaper at four-years-old, because I had so thoroughly messed up. I think I can trace other areas of life with him that are difficult, to this same kind of thinking on my part. Thankfully my partner stepped in and took care of guiding the others when they were ready."

Natural Rhythm
"I don't have any memories, but my mother had a daycare while I was growing up and I watched as dozens and dozens of kids were toilet-trained throughout the years. It was such a natural process that unfolded as the kids were ready. I was able to hold onto that belief and used my experience to guide my decisions with my children. Thankfully, my partner was completely open and supportive."

Petrifying and Paralyzing Pressure
"I don't remember being toilet-trained, but I do remember wetting the bed until I was 11-years-old. It was such a humiliating experience. My mother would try to influence me by telling me how disappointed and hurt she was that I was doing this to her. It is the reason our relationship is still so tense and strained. Both my partner and I work, and so we need to have our kids toilet-trained by three-years-old so they can go to preschool and we can save money on childcare. This underlying pressure freaks me out, because I know what an emotional issue this is for all involved. I am petrified, and having no idea how to move forward, I am completely paralyzed. This would be a great place for my partner and I to work together to create a healthy parenting plan."

Managing a Milestone
"I am an older mom, who had trouble getting pregnant. Finally, at 46-years-old, I am faced with the challenge of toilet-training. I have watched my friends and family go through this, and it

has been such a different experience for each one of them. I've learned that each child is unique and has his or her own path. I hope I am able to keep this point of view when I actually reach that milestone. My partner is twelve years older than I am and used to being in charge of his schedule. He is worried that everything we have planned out will be impacted by our child's progress with potty-training. I thought we could just deal with this as it came up, but I see that we need to put a plan in place otherwise my laid-back nature and his need to be in control will cause problems for all of us."

Rewards Are Punishments

"I am the oldest of four siblings. I basically potty-trained the other three kids. Piece of cake as far as I am concerned; my partner on the other hand does not like messes, refuses to allow the children to run around without a diaper, and insists that times have changed and there are better ways now, using rewards and punishment to train kids how to use the toilet. We are so different in our perspectives that I am afraid we won't be able to work together at all. His ideas make me shudder."

Cycle of Control

"I used to hold my bowel movements to prove to my parents that they could not control me. I still am so resentful that I find ways to demonstrate to them, that I am in charge of myself. I don't realize I am doing it most times. When it comes to my children, I get so highly charged around sleeping, eating and bathroom issues, because I know that these areas are where kids have the final say. I am so worried that I will inadvertently repeat the cycle. I think my high anxiety is causing anxiety for all of us. Instead of worrying about potty-training, I need to figure out how to calm myself and not create problems that don't exist."

Exercise Two: A Vision for the Future

Using what you have discovered, write your vision for the future, including any action items you will incorporate into daily life with your family.

Here are some examples from clients to help illustrate this exercise.

Setting the Pace
"I am going to let my children set the timeline. When they are ready, they are ready. Their signals could be fighting diaper changes, talking to me about going the bathroom, staying dry until I change them. Whatever they are, I will be on the lookout and hope to notice and facilitate this process calmly and at their pace."

Supporting Role
"My partner is home all day with the children, so I will do whatever she decides. She is going to be leading the charge here with the kids, and I will check in with her to make sure that I am supporting her efforts in the way she would like me to."

Exercise Three: Intersect, Parallel, Diverge

When you and your partner revisit this section, you will have a chance to share your experiences and move forward in creating a shared vision and a parenting plan to support that vision.

Based on your experiences do you believe this is an area where you and your partner I (intersect), P (run parallel) or D (diverge)? Circle the best identifying category.

Bedtime and Sleeping Habits

There are many methods available to parents as they research the best way to support healthy sleeping habits in their children. Depending on the philosophy you ascribe to and your personal set of values, you may let them cry it out, you may bring them into a family bed or you may be available for them to nurse on demand. Whatever method you select, you will likely experience success if you remain consistent and you and your partner agree on the method. If you don't agree on a method—or worse, you have no plan at all—it's likely you will make rash decisions in the moment that confuse the child and complicate your ability to create a plan that you can both execute over the course of many weeks.

Prompt

It's 7:00 p.m. Maybe you are already in your pajamas or you are reading a book with your mom. Maybe you are still running around the house and one of your parents keeps telling you it's almost time for bed. Think of as many details as you can that capture what the bedtime routine looked like for you growing up. Capture the feel of it. Were you stressed or relaxed, did you fight going to bed or were you ready to settle in when it was time? Once you were in bed, could you fall asleep easily, or did you fidget and squirm and get out of bed several times to check on mom and dad? Perhaps you shared a room or a bed with a sibling. How did your parents deal with you when you cried out, or got out of bed several times or woke up in the middle of the night? What is the overall feeling you have about bedtime and sleeping when you were a child?

Exercise One: Self-Discovery

Write a brief statement capturing your childhood experiences and memories surrounding bedtime. Then capture a belief or decision you made and finish with any *aha* moments or new insights.

Here are a few examples from parents who completed the exercise.

Motivated by Fear

Impressions from Childhood

"My parents were very attentive and playful throughout the day. At bedtime, they became more serious. We had 15-minutes for whatever it was we had to accomplish. If we were quick and brushed our teeth and changed into our pajamas quickly, we would have time for one story or song. I always felt rushed, and like they couldn't wait to get rid of us at the end of the day. I wanted to provide my children with a bit more time to relax and let go of the day's events."

From Past to Present
"I didn't want my kids to have that same rushed feeling I had or to ever think I was trying to get rid of them, so I think I decided to do things very differently when I had kids, and that is about as much thought as I gave it. Or perhaps I imagined some magical bedtime routine but had no idea how I would execute it."

Insight
"The big *aha* moment for me is that I have trouble setting boundaries, and I am up and down the stairs for thirty minutes to maybe an hour, bringing water, looking under the bed for monsters, checking in the closet, or adjusting the fan. It is exhausting and cuts into time I could be spending with my partner at night. I was making parenting decisions out of fear instead of really considering the importance of a consistent, thoughtful bedtime routine."

No Nighttime Routine

Impressions from Childhood
"Bedtime routine? There was no such thing at my house. For as far back as I can remember, my parents said, 'It is time for bed,' and we got up from whatever it was we were doing and kissed them and marched upstairs. I am sure when I was very little, they helped us brush our teeth and get into our pajamas, but I have no memory of that."

From Past to Present
"I don't think I ever considered doing it any other way when I had kids."

Insight
"I found myself getting annoyed with my own kids when they refused to go upstairs and get ready for bed on their own, and kept insisting that they needed help, which I knew they didn't.

Truthfully bedtimes suck, and if things don't change, it's going to be rough on all of us."

Decompress and Prepare

"My father worked long hours and came home just before we went to sleep. The routine was that we would eat with my mother, she would finish preparing his dinner and he would swoop upstairs to put my sister and me in bed. We would laugh, snuggle and read. It always lasted twenty minutes, no more and no less. It was individual, undivided attention and my most favorite part of the day. Still to this day, my personal bedtime routine is the highlight of my day—decompressing and preparing for a night of restful sleep. I don't know how to maintain my preference and my time and also give my children the same experience that I had. I tried deferring this responsibility to my partner, but she thinks I should participate in some way. I am just not sure how to support the routine without sacrificing my own. I need this time to function the next day."

Loving Ritual

"Bedtime was a loving ritual for me when I was growing up. My mother stayed at home and seemed to have everything taken care of and under control. I had the perfect childhood all the way around, and that included my bedtime. My mother was always there for me and always had time. How she did it, I'll never understand. Both my partner and I work long hours. When we finally get home after working, picking the kids up from daycare and afterschool programs, helping with homework, making dinner, eating, cleaning up and preparing for the next day, we are wiped out. I can't keep going like this, doing everything. We don't really have a routine. We do it all and the only way we can get our kids to sleep is to lay down with them. One of us inevitably ends up sleeping the night in bed with one of our children, if not both of us, waking in the morning coming out of each of their rooms. This is no way to live, and it is taking a toll on our marriage. We need help, but I have no idea where to start."

Independently Navigated

"From the time we were young, my parents set out to teach us how to take care of ourselves, and bedtime was no different. We were connected and loved and supported by our parents. If we were scared at night, my parents were there, but we were taught to navigate our bedtime routines independently and call them when we were ready for a kiss good-night. I decided to create this for my children a well. My partner is on board and we have some hiccups every now and again, but basically bedtime rocks for us."

Exercise Two: A Vision for the Future

Using what you have discovered, write your vision for the future, including any action items you will incorporate into daily life with your family.

Here are some examples from clients to help illustrate this exercise.

Routines and Boundaries

"Time to set some boundaries. I have faith in my children's abilities to navigate the bedtime routine without me so it's time to step out. My partner and I need to spend some time outlining a simple routine for the kids and let them practice. I think we also need to set some boundaries and create habits for ourselves. Make a plan and get really clear about what we will do and will not do in terms of bedtime support."

Exercise Three: Intersect, Parallel, Diverge

When you and your partner revisit this section, you will have a chance to share your experiences and move forward in creating a shared vision and a parenting plan to support that vision.

Based on your experiences do you believe this is an area where you and your partner I (intersect), P (run parallel) or D (diverge)? Circle the best identifying category.

Routines

There is no longer any doubt that routines in our lives help create and maintain balance, consistency, continuity, security and the ability to remain present in our busy lives. They help with procrastination, prioritizing, and goal setting. We know now that children thrive in an environment where there are established routines that help them organize their day and can minimize stress and anxiety. Sometimes routines can become too rigid and work against us, and at other times, our need for spontaneity can create chaos and confusion.

Prompt

Consider your own childhood and whether or not there were established routines when you were growing up. How did you wake up in the morning? Who woke you up, and was it the same way each day? What about breakfast and getting dressed and ready for school? Was there a routine that kept the family moving forward, or did you play it by ear each day? Did you have any after-school routines, like a snack around the table and then homework, or playing outside until it was dark and homework after dinner? Then there is evening and bedtime. Did you have any rituals like getting your clothes laid out for the following day or taking a bath and visiting with a parent? Consider all the routines that might have gone unnoticed by a child, but as an adult, you can see their influence clearly. Think back on any conversations you might have had with your parents about routines and how they fit into your daily life.

Exercise One: Self-Discovery

Write a brief statement capturing your childhood experiences and memories surrounding routines. Then capture a belief or decision you made and finish with any *aha* moments or new insights.

Here are a few examples from parents who completed the exercise.

Overcompensating Causes Anxiety

Impressions from Childhood
"My family was constantly running from one task to the next. Both of my parents worked odd shifts at the hospital, and I never knew who was going to be home when I got home from school or who would be there when I woke up. Each one had a different way of doing things, and we adjusted for sure, but I never knew how the day would start or end. They were also so busy that our things were everywhere and our house was a mess."

From Past to Present
"I firmly believe that people operate better when life is organized, and for me that means there is a place for everything and everything is in its place. I believe that when you have routines established and the kids know what to expect, everyone is happier and can concentrate on important things, rather than on finding their stuff or trying to figure out what happens next."

Insight
"As I watch my oldest head into elementary school, I recognize that he has a difficult time being flexible and adjusting to life when things don't go according to plan. He has a high level of anxiety, and it comes out as whining and clinging. I think in my attempt to provide structure and eliminate anxiety, I have created some of it."

Freedom with Structure
"I grew up living on a small family farm, so there was always something to do. My parents also each held full-time jobs, so the responsibilities fell on my two brothers and me to take care of much of the work. We had very structured routines, because the animals and the vegetables could not wait. We had to be efficient and effective in order to keep up with the farm and our education. My best friend's family was so laid back and free spirited. No rules about bedtime, mealtime, hygiene or homework. Life was all about having fun. You just did what you did and that was okay. My friend and I used to talk about how different our

fathers were and that if we could mix them into one person, we would have the perfect parent. Both of them loved us, but we craved a balance. I decided that I would offer my kids freedom with structure. I think I am doing a great job, but my partner often disagrees and thinks there should be more structure. This is a place we could work better together, and I think if we can find some common ground, we could create a really great atmosphere for everyone."

Sense of Order

"I never gave routines a second thought growing up. Looking back I realize that they gave our lives a sense of order without being restrictive. For instance, dinner was always at 7:00 p.m., because my dad got home on the train by 6:30 p.m., had his cocktail and then we ate, but if he had a good day, we could go out and celebrate with dinner and stay out late, even on a school night. I wanted my kids to have special memories, and so I think we make concessions to routines too often. For example, many times they ask to stay up late, and we just let them because it is easier than fighting with them. Then they are tired after three late nights, and we end up fighting anyway. We could benefit from routines, but first my partner and I need to figure out how to stay firm with our kids so they can learn the routines."

Routines for Fun

"I remember routines as a kid, although I wouldn't have called them that when I was young. We knew that Friday nights were movie and pizza nights, and we could count on it weekly. Sundays we went to church and stopped for a donut on the way there. We knew that bedtime was a five-minute foot rub and then kiss good-night. I think these routines helped keep me feeling secure, because no matter what was said during the day, for instance, I knew that my mom would rub my feet before I drifted off to sleep. I love routines. I set them up for fun things to look forward to and ways to get things done during the day. My partner thinks that I am too rigid and have too many expectations around routines. We differ and argue about this quite a bit. I don't want to back down."

Practice the Process

"I loved routines as a kid. Routines meant predictability. I was organized and knew where all my stuff was and I was always prepared. I am a firm believer in routines and set them for my kids. The problem is I haven't taken into account their own personal preferences and rhythms. I have routines around homework and have a child that insists she can get up before school and has begged us to let her try it. I have a hard time trusting her, and my husband and I don't see eye-to-eye on this issue. He wonders why I am making such a big deal about it and wants to let her try it before we say no. I am not sure about it, but now I wonder, what if it worked? If I want my kids to be as good at setting up routines as I am, they need to be part of the process and practice."

Exercise Two: A Vision for the Future

Using what you have discovered, write your vision for the future, including any action items you will incorporate into daily life with your family.

Here are some examples from clients to help illustrate this exercise.

Routines Supporting Preferences

"Routines are an integral part of our family dynamic, but the ones I put in place are not always the best for my own children with their unique personalities and preferences. I will work with each one of them to help develop routines that support their individual natures."

Routines Guiding Responsibility

"Routines are important and help us navigate our busy lives with ease; however, I tend to be inflexible. I will decide with my partner which routines we can shake up a bit to provide some room for our children to let their hair down a bit and eventually take on more responsibility."

Exercise Three: Intersect, Parallel, Diverge

When you and your partner revisit this section, you will have a chance to share your experiences and move forward in creating a shared vision and a parenting plan to support that vision.

Based on your experiences, do you believe this is an area where you and your partner I (intersect), P (run parallel) or D (diverge)? Circle the best identifying category.

Technology

We all have our own beliefs about technology. How much? How little? When? Where? Safety? Monitored? Unmonitored? Depending upon when you were born or your current career path, your beliefs and ideas on technology can be very different. Do you make your decisions based on the scary statistics and nightmare stories from your friends, or from sound research and your own experience with a new device or app? Keeping up with this fast paced industry can either excite or overwhelm a parent. The bottom line is we all have a story that influences our parenting decisions when it comes to technology and our kids. Whether you are a young parent and your phone is your key to navigating daily life, or you are older and still have trouble navigating email, you are challenged with introducing technology to your kids in a way that works for the entire family.

Prompt
The digital age and all its technology is here, and it's here to stay. Chances are you have very firm ideas about the use of technology in your home and how you will approach this area of life with your kids. You and partner could be on the same page, and one of you might still be bragging that they are the only adult they know without a cell phone. Take a moment and consider what is influencing your current parenting practices when it comes to technology. If you are an older parent, you won't necessarily have any childhood memories about technology, but it's likely that there was something "new" when you were growing up and

you watched as your parents navigated a new challenge in their lives as parents.

Exercise One: Self-Discovery

Write a brief statement capturing your childhood experiences and memories surrounding technology use. Then capture a belief or decision you made and finish with any *aha* moments or new insights.

Here are a few examples from parents who completed the exercise.

Setting Strict Guidelines
"I am in my fifties and joke with my kids about the video games we used to play. I think playing outside and being active is so very important. I don't understand the appeal of sitting around all day and watching a screen. We set strict guidelines about how much and when and where our kids can access their screens. I don't think there is any harm in this and I do not want to back down."

Resource for Learning
"I teach Tech Ed to elementary school aged kids. I love it. Technology can offer us so much. I don't think there is anything wrong with it at all. How is reading any different from watching YouTube to teach yourself how to fix a car or make a cake or braid your hair? We have access to so much information that will change our lives. I say some kids are more open to being active, and some like to soak up all the information they can. I know as with anything there are risks, and if we monitor our children to make sure they are being safe, I don't think there needs to be limits. My wife disagrees. It is a point of contention. We are constantly showing each other articles to prove our points and support our way of thinking. It is a battle, and come to think of it, I have no idea how my kids feel about it. That might be the first place to start. Maybe they will provide some middle ground."

Special Treat

"Technology was not available to us as kids the way it is today, but we did have a television growing up and it was available to us on Saturday nights only. It was a special treat that we experienced together as a family. This makes sense to me. I want the technology in our home to be a treat, not something that we use to disconnect from each other. I am so afraid that my kids will disappear into their rooms each with their own personal device. We share two phones among the four of us (one for the kids and one for the parents.) We have one computer and one television both in the open areas. I have heard from my friends that when my children are at their homes, all they want to do is watch television or browse the web. I don't know what to do because it goes against everything I believe to be right."

Maintain Healthy Balance

"Technology is part of our lives. We must learn to incorporate it into our lives in a healthy and balanced way. I know that too much of anything is not a good thing, but I don't want to deprive my children of what is available to us, only to have them go crazy with it once I can no longer control what they do when they are not here with us. I want them to be screen smart, so I am going to let them make mistakes and practice and master this life skill."

No Middle Ground

"Getting ahead in today's world requires a confidence with technology. If I want my kids to be successful, they must be comfortable and adept with technology. As with anything, this requires practice. Our challenge is how much is enough? I want to set boundaries, and my spouse wants to let the kids decide. We can't agree, so we do nothing except fight about it."

Battle of Wills

"I think technology is going to be the demise of our society. It is banned from our home. The kids have access at school where it is monitored. I won't pay for it or support the use of it. I won't discuss it. I am set. My wife does not agree, and she has been arming the kids with arguments against me. We might get divorced over this issue."

Social Sidekick
"I refer to my phone as my sidekick. I love it. I love connecting with my kids on their social apps. It is part of life, and if I can't temper my use, why should I ask my kids to? We do have guidelines like no phones at the table or in church or at a restaurant, but we have so much fun watching funny videos and looking at memes. It's great. I figure if I don't focus on the scary parts, they won't notice. My husband thinks we are too connected to our devices and tries to suggest that we put them down every now and again, but we don't listen to him. He feels like his opinion does not matter."

Exercise Two: A Vision for the Future

Using what you have discovered, write your vision for the future, including any action items you will incorporate into daily life with your family.

Here are some examples from clients to help illustrate this exercise.

Balanced Activities
"I think that my adolescent-aged daughter is too dependent on her phone. I would like to set goals for when, where, and how often we all use our technology. I firmly believe we must all do at least one thing active each day in an effort to balance out the time we spend on our screens."

Willing to Compromise
"Technology goes against all that I believe in, but I am the parent of three middle-school-aged children. My wife seems to have a handle on what all the other kids are doing these days and what is safe and healthy. I am going to ask that my children are not on their devices around me, but will acknowledge that they have agreements with their mother, and if I have a question, I will

check in with her, instead of passing judgment or attacking my children."

Exercise Three: Intersect, Parallel, Diverge

When you and your partner revisit this section, you will have a chance to share your experiences and move forward in creating a shared vision and a parenting plan to support that vision.

Based on your experiences, do you believe this is an area where you and your partner I (intersect), P (run parallel) or D (diverge)? Circle the best identifying category.

Money

Not only is money a sensitive subject for couples; it can be a point of contention when it comes to money and our kids. Your own childhood experiences as well as your current relationship with money will influence your beliefs and thus your parenting decisions. Remember that money will be a part of our children's lives forever, so it's important that you get clear on your attitudes, beliefs and decisions.

Not all parents have the same goals when it comes to money and kids. Some parents want their kids to learn through experience and might provide weekly allowance to accomplish this. Others might want to put restrictions on the money their children have access to and monitor how they spend their money, while others might want to ensure their kids never go without. Remember, there is no right or wrong in parenting, just your views, so be open to exploring other perspectives in order to find a balance between opposing views.

Prompt

Think back to when you were a young child, perhaps between the ages of five and ten years old, and consider how your parents dealt with money. When you have several memories regarding money, notice if there are themes, attitudes or words that best capture what it meant to have money or not have enough money each month to pay the bills or to put money away for emergencies or college. What did your parents say about people who had money, and what did they say about people who did not? What messages did your parents communicate to you about being responsible with money? Did they have biases toward those who saved or those who spent? Did money give your family security or was it the cause of fighting between your parents? Was happiness connected to money? Was money the root of all evil? Was there enough or never enough? Were there systems and budgets in place or did it grow on trees? You are bound to recall all kinds of memories around money once you focus in on the subject. Gather as much information as you can without editing it and remember, no judging, and then capture those memories.

Exercise One: Self-Discovery

Write a brief statement capturing your childhood experiences and memories surrounding money. Then capture a belief or decision you made and finish with any *aha* moments or new insights.

Here are a few examples from parents who completed the exercise.

Point of Contention
"My parents got me whatever I wanted, and I never gave money much thought until I got older. Then reality hit and I had to learn quickly how to budget and that I wouldn't be able to afford the things my parents provided. I don't have a plan, so I bounce all over the place. This might explain why my partner and I argue about this topic regularly. Money is one of those areas of life that you have to keep talking about with your kids and flushing out where you and your partner have similar ideas and where you don't. We have so much talking to do on this issue if we want to set our kids up for success."

Overwhelmed and Derailed
"We were strapped for cash growing up, so I learned not to ask for anything and not expect anything. I definitely developed a scarcity mind-set around money. I didn't want my kids to worry

about money and develop a scarcity mind-set like me so when they were young, I got them whatever they needed or wanted. My thinking was that there would be plenty of time for them to earn their own. I am beginning to rethink this decision. It is based solely on my own experience and not on sound research about teaching kids about finances. My partner and I avoid conversations that have to do with budgeting, saving and finances in general, and I think that is because I get defensive and overwhelmed and the conversation gets derailed."

Money Management 101

"I was given an allowance when I was young and learned quickly about money management. By the time I was in high school I had a good job, and other than the necessities my parents provided, I was responsible for any extras I wanted and to pay for my own car, phone and so on. I want my kids to have a healthy relationship with money and time to practice learning how to spend it, save it and budget. I will have to make sure they have access to money regularly and set guidelines we can all live with and that are age appropriate."

Weekly Allowance

"My dad was in finance so we spent a lot of time talking about money when I was young. I felt like I had a good sense of how money worked, the value of it, what it could and could not do for you in life. I decided I would give my kids allowance each week and let them spend it as they see fit, so they get lots of experience learning to save, spend and give it away while they are young. My partner and I see eye to eye in this area of life with the kids, and now I realize that because we are on the same page, the kids really trust us when we talk about money."

Financially Responsible

"My parents were completely irresponsible, and it was not unusual to find the electricity turned off because they didn't pay the bill. They made excuses and said that life was for living, not for worrying about how much money you had in the bank. I was embarrassed, ashamed and scared to death that one day we wouldn't have a house to come home to. I believe kids should have to work for money, and I let them earn a little by doing chores, or getting good grades so they know how hard it is to come by and how easily it disappears and will never take anything for granted. My partner and I disagree, but because I refuse to budge on my stance, we can't ever have a conversation that opens up other ways of teaching the kids. It has become a real sore spot for us. I don't know if I can see things differently, but I am willing to consider it if I think it will help the kids learn about responsible finances."

Exercise Two: A Vision for the Future

Using what you have discovered, write your vision for the future, including any action items you will incorporate into daily life with your family.

Here are some examples from clients to help illustrate this exercise.

Healthy Relationship

"A healthy relationship with money, what it can and cannot do, how to use it to add value and meaning to your life and how to act responsibly with it is my new goal for teaching my kids about money. This is a far cry from *my money doesn't grow on trees* and *I am not an ATM machine* lectures. Having a plan that is based on facts rather than on your own childhood experience is the smarter way to go."

Letting Go

"I have to give up control in this area. I have been making things worse instead of preparing my kids for the huge responsibility of managing money. My partner has a very common sense approach to finances, and instead of leveraging his confidence and sensible attitude, I have found reasons to work against him. Time for a new game plan and I will follow his lead."

Exercise Three: Intersect, Parallel, Diverge

When you and your partner revisit this section, you will have a chance to share your experiences and move forward in creating a shared vision and a parenting plan to support that vision.

Based on your experiences, do you believe this is an area where you and your partner I (intersect), P (run parallel) or D (diverge)? Circle the best identifying category.

Additional Topics for Exploration

As mentioned, here are other areas of day-to-day life for you to consider. By now, you understand the process of examining childhood memories, capturing a few that are most representative of your experience, and then reflecting on how those experiences became decisions that influence your current parenting practices, and during this examination, you may have experienced an *aha* moment that brought more clarity to a current situation. Use this same process with any of these topics, or others that I haven't mentioned here.

- ◆ Extracurricular activities
- ◆ Nurse or bottle feed
- ◆ Sleepovers
- ◆ Dances
- ◆ Boy-girl parties
- ◆ Curfews
- ◆ Parties
- ◆ Dating
- ◆ Decorating your room
- ◆ Hygiene
- ◆ Personal style
- ◆ Traditions
- ◆ Birthdays
- ◆ Religious holidays
- ◆ Celebrations

When you have completed Exercises One and Two, return to this chapter with your partner and find where your experiences intersect, run parallel or diverge, and then begin to construct a thoughtful parenting plan that will guide your decision-making process for years to come. You can find the instructions for writing your Parenting Plan in Chapter 7.

6

Lifestyle

In this chapter, you are going to explore areas of your childhood that impact your ideas on discipline, emotional health, education and more. These areas I refer to as your lifestyle. They are broader more general topics, rather than the specifics of technology and toilet-training. These topics are often intertwined with each other and show up in daily life, but define who we are in a bigger picture view.

Just like in Chapters 4 and 5, each section is designed to elicit memories and emotions so you can tap into the decisions you made that are impacting your parenting practices today and either contributing to a cooperative or contentious relationship with your partner.

Instructions

Complete Exercise One on your own. After reading through the prompts, recall your early childhood memories and impressions, the decisions you made based on those memories and any *aha* moments or insight as a result of your exploration.

Complete Exercise Two on your own. Write a vision for how you would like things to be going forward. It's possible you may want to make minor adjustments or you understand that a complete overhaul is in order. You and your partner will share the vision for the future and determine if your ideas, views and perspectives intersect, run parallel or diverge.

Complete Exercise Three with your partner. After sharing your memories and your new vision for the future, decide with your partner if you think this is an area where your ideas, views and perspective, intersect, run parallel or diverge, so when you are ready to write a parenting plan together, you can begin your work in the areas of life where you intersect.

Discipline

The following statements are meant to spark specific experiences, as well as a general overall impression of how discipline was handled in your home. It's easy to generalize this category with statements like *my parents were pretty fair, my parents were super strict, I knew better than to cross my father*, or *my mom was a softy*. Take time to flush out as many specific examples of how discipline was handled when you were growing up. Some of the statements may seem harsh, but your response to them will tell you more about yourself and your overall thoughts and feelings about discipline and children, if you answer them honestly. Later, you and your partner will begin to explore your experiences, and together create an approach to discipline that you can both support if your aim is to raise emotionally healthy, respectful and responsible children. For now, focus on you and your own early experiences.

Exercise One: Self-Discovery

Circle all the statements that best represent the discipline style used by your parents. Remember, this is based on facts, not on how you wish things had been. Believe it or not, we all have a preferred style, whether it's more authoritarian, permissive or democratic. Right now, you are gathering information that will support you and your partner as you create a mutually agreed upon approach to discipline. For this to be possible, you must identify your triggers, understand how you are making decisions regarding discipline and be willing to work with your partner to form a united front that incorporates both of your ideas and goals.

Restrictive, Controlling

This style of parenting doesn't necessarily mean that your parents were mean, cruel or unkind. It does, however, indicate a strong parental desire to make the rules and enforce the rules. Your parents believed that this was in your best interest, and that they would be negligent in their parental responsibility, if you were not punished accordingly.

- My parents threatened and punished me when I made mistakes.
- My parents rewarded me if I was "good" or behaved well.
- My parents used time-outs, naughty chairs, counting and threatening when I misbehaved.
- My parents believed yelling at me would get me to understand and do what they wanted.
- When I got older, my parents threatened to take away privileges or things that were important to me (friends, computer time, television, sports).
- My parents thought making me feel bad, ashamed or guilty would make me behave better the next time.
- My parents had high expectations and often used disappointment in an effort to motivate me to perform to their standards.
- My parents made me apologize when I misbehaved.
- I stopped trusting my parents when I got to middle school.
- My parents made the discipline harsher than it needed to be.
- I ignored my parents' attempts to discipline me.
- I tried to avoid getting in trouble because I was afraid of my parents.
- I often felt hopeless in my attempts to be "good" and finally resigned myself to the punishments they doled out.

- I fought back by shouting, insulting or swearing at my parents.
- My parents expected strict obedience to their rules.

_____ Number of statements you agree with

Unstructured, Permissive, Laissez-Faire

This style of parenting doesn't necessarily mean your parents were complete pushovers and gave into your every whim and demand. It can, however, indicate that they were able to excuse and overlook, rather than correct behaviors. Your parents could have had difficulty setting and maintaining boundaries that helped to support the healthy development of your habits.

- My parents threatened to punish me but rarely did.
- I could talk my parents out of punishing me or letting me do something they told me I couldn't do.
- My parents would often overlook my misbehavior or make excuses for me.
- My parents might have lectured me about my behavior, but they rarely did anything about it.
- My parents didn't yell because they knew I would get upset, and they didn't want that.
- My parents weren't sure how to discipline me.
- When my parents did something to correct misbehavior, I ignored it.
- If one parent was too harsh, the other parent would console me or try and make me feel better.
- I could easily manipulate my parents into overlooking my misbehavior.
- My parents seemed uncomfortable and uncertain when they disciplined me.
- I got away with too much.
- My parents rarely followed through on what they said they would do.
- My parents wanted me to like them.

_____ Number of statements you agree with

Moderate, Democratic, Leaders

This style of parenting recognizes that treating children with dignity and respect, setting firm and realistic boundaries, offering choices and following through on what is said ensures children will grow up with a strong sense of right and wrong, with the courage to take responsibility for mistakes, make amends when necessary and learn from experience. The majority of the time your parents were consistent, level-headed and reasonable, they believed that you were capable and had faith in your ability to navigate your life with guidance and support.

- ◆ My parents tried to redirect my behavior toward something productive if I was misbehaving.
- ◆ My parents tried to model the behavior they wanted to see in their kids.
- ◆ My parents let me experience the consequences of my misbehavior, good and bad.
- ◆ My parents were fair in their discipline.
- ◆ I knew what behaviors my parents expected from me.
- ◆ My parents made the consequences of misbehavior clear to me.
- ◆ My parents acted as a unified front when disciplining me.
- ◆ My parents talked to me about what I did.
- ◆ I knew I was loved even when being disciplined.
- ◆ My parents viewed my misbehavior as part of the learning process.
- ◆ I trusted my parents and knew that they were trying to be fair when they disciplined me.
- ◆ My parents followed through on what they said.

_____ Number of statements you agree with

Write a brief statement capturing your childhood experiences and memories surrounding discipline. Then capture a belief or decision you made and finish with any *aha* moments or new insights.

Here are a few examples from parents who completed the exercise.

Paralyzed by Decisions

Impressions from Childhood
"My mother and father were at odds with each other over how to discipline their kids. If one was too hard, the other was too easy, and then they would switch. It left me feeling uneasy and scared every time I got into trouble."

From Past to Present
"I want my partner and I to be on the same page at least 90% of the time, and I decided the best way to accomplish this was to never make a decision without first consulting him. Instead of this creating a unified house, it causes stress because we never seem to be able to make any decisions, and our kids are left hanging or nothing ever happens."

Insight
"Our children know that I am paralyzed when it comes to making decisions. They know that they can get away with anything because I never act. By the time my husband and I discuss the matter, too much time has passed. You'd think by now we'd have a plan, but we treat each incident in isolation. I am exhausted. I think I am making it more difficult than it has to be."

Harsh Parenting

Impressions from Childhood
"My mom and dad were able to agree on their discipline strategies, but they were always too harsh for what I did, and I did everything I could to avoid getting into trouble."

From Past to Present
"I did not want my children to grow up making decisions based on fear. I wanted them to make decisions based on what supported who they were as people. Whenever my partner uses harsh discipline strategies, I come to my children's defense."

Insight

"My kids view us (as parents) as the good parent and the bad parent. They are always pitting us against each other. They play us, and it is causing a huge rift in our marriage."

Lack of Boundaries

Impressions from Childhood

"I really wished my parents had created some boundaries and expectations of us as kids. They overlooked a lot of my trouble-making or acted like it was no big deal. Looking back on it now, I realize I always felt a bit anxious and uncertain. I think I would have benefited from more rules and boundaries."

From Past to Present

"I was not going to let my kids feel this anxiety. I set boundaries and they must be followed. This is all in the best interest of my children."

Insight

"I have a huge reaction when my partner allows my children certain freedoms or second chances. I do not want to be a wishy-washy parent and feel like my partner is sabotaging my goals to raise decent human beings. Otherwise, we can work together well."

Outcome of Consequences

"If I messed up, my mom would dish out a reasonable consequence and leave me to clean up my mess. It taught me to think before I acted. I appreciated the freedom within the boundaries that my parents offered us as kids and wanted to provide the same environment for my children. It takes time but it works. My partner said she wanted this too, but the reality is that she is afraid that the outcome won't be a good one and the process will take too long. We agree on what we want, but the path to get there creates problems."

Lectures Lack Follow-Through

"I sat through daily lectures on what I did wrong and what I should do next time, but nothing ever happened so I just kept doing what I wanted. I decided that I would do things differently when I was raising my children. I wasn't going to lecture or use the line, *because I said so*. The problem is that when chaos ensues, I fall back into habits I learned from my parents. I said I wouldn't do the same thing as my parents, when I became a parent, but I never identified exactly what I would do. My partner and I are at odds, because I turn into the crazy person that we decided we would never be with our children. I need to identify some tools and practice them with the support of my partner."

Ineffective Parenting Strategies

"Time-outs, naughty chairs, counting, sticker charts, money jars, you name it, my parents tried it with me. To tell you the truth, I didn't pay any attention to them until they got mad and yelled at me, and then I was reduced to tears and they felt bad. I was so confused, but I remember thinking that if you cried, people would let you off the hook. I entered into parenthood knowing that all of these strategies were not very effective, but had no idea what else to do, so I used them. Truthfully I didn't give it much thought. Now I understand that this job takes thought and intention. I can't wing it and be effective. My poor kids don't know what to expect from me. I am all over the place and I see why I drive my spouse crazy."

Shame and Control

"My parents were controlling and used punishment and shame to try and keep me in line. The more they came down on me, the harder I rebelled. I went the other way, of course, and decided I would *never* punish or shame my own kids. Instead I negotiate, I change my mind based on my moods, and I give in. I thought my decision on how to discipline differently would make for a relaxed family, but just the opposite is true. The kids never know from one day to the next what to expect, and I lose confidence in my ability to discipline in an effective way. I expect my partner to support my decisions around discipline, but I change the rules so often he can't keep track and we end up in a fight."

Battle of Wills

"My mother was so wishy-washy that I never experienced any consequences in my life, which made early adulthood hell for me. As a result, I decided that as a parent, I would have a strong, firm, rule-based home to raise my kids in. As soon as my oldest child turned two, the battle of wills began. Not only did my relationship with him suffer, but my partner, who came from a very restrictive home, found it impossible to back me up and tried to protect our son from my wrath."

Effective Role Models

"My parents were pretty low key, but consistent and firm in their handling of discipline. I decided to incorporate their style into my own parenting. I learned how to help my kids reflect on what they had done and what they might do differently in the future, and my partner who came from a similar home agreed, and we are able to work together, support each other and offer assistance if one of us was feeling overwhelmed or highly charged by something the kids did."

Exercise Two: A Vision for the Future

Using what you have discovered, write your vision for the future, including any action items you will incorporate into daily life with your family.

Here are some examples from clients to help illustrate this exercise.

Eliminate Idle Threats

"I would like to be more consistent and provide stability for my children. This means that I will have to stay calm, even when my blood is boiling and not yell out idle threats. If I need to leave the room and calm down before addressing my children I will. This sounds so easy, but it is really hard for me. My partner has a much better time of this, and the kids respond well to his taking a break and getting control of his emotions. I have never asked him to help me get better at this, but I think I can put my ego aside and ask him now."

Following Through

"It is important to me to follow-through so my children know they can trust me. This means when we make an agreement, I need to follow through no matter what antics my children employ to break down my confidence. I think I need a mantra to remind me that following through shows respect for myself and for the kids, so I don't get tripped up with their attempts to manipulate me into giving in."

Exercise Three: Intersect, Parallel, Diverge

When you and your partner revisit this section, you will have a chance to share your experiences from Exercise One and Two and then move forward in creating a shared vision and a parenting plan to support that vision.

Based on your experiences, do you believe this is an area where you and your partner I (intersect), P (run parallel) or D (diverge)? Circle the best identifying category.

Emotional Health

Most of the parents I know and work with are committed to providing their children with healthy nutritional options. They buy organic produce and groceries, minimize sugar and processed food, encourage exercise and outside play as well as provide time for rest. Many parents have even introduced mindful or meditative techniques to their children. The focus is primarily on keeping our children physically healthy, and I applaud the efforts. Equally essential is our children's emotional health, and yet most parents I talk with struggle to explain how they are actively supporting the emotional health of their kids. In fact, because emotional health is not tangible and not often quantifiable, it can be difficult for parents to not only know what to do, but understand how to come to an agreement about how to go about supporting healthy emotional development with their partner.

A useful definition of emotional well-being and a great place to start is offered by the Mental Health Foundation: "A positive sense of well-being which enables an individual to be able to function in society and meet the demands of everyday life; people in good mental health have the ability to recover effectively from illness, change or misfortune."

Circle the statements that best capture your childhood experiences. Add your own if necessary.

- ◆ My parents believed pointing out my flaws would get me to improve.
- ◆ My parents focused on my strengths and encouraged me to focus on my progress rather than on demanding perfection.
- ◆ My parents used positive words like smart, strong, respectful, flexible, compassionate, honest, truthful, hardworking, productive, focused, kind, forgiving, and accepting to describe me.
- ◆ My parents used negative words like dumb, stupid, slow, fidgety, unfocused, lazy, cruel, demanding, bossy, snotty, rude, disrespectful and selfish to describe me.
- ◆ Expectations were clear, reasonable, and realistic.
- ◆ Expectations were unclear, unreasonable, and unrealistic.
- ◆ My parents were consistent and fair, and I felt secure and understood.
- ◆ My parents were inconsistent and unnecessarily hard on me, and I was tense and nervous.
- ◆ My parents supported my interests and talked with me about them.
- ◆ My parents did not seem interested in my life.
- ◆ I felt comfortable expressing negative emotions.
- ◆ I felt a strong sense of belonging and significance within my family.
- ◆ I felt as if I was a disappointment to my parents and the cause of their frustration.

- One or both of my parents were emotionally volatile with each other and with me.
- My negative feelings made one or both of my parents uncomfortable.
- One or both of my parents were often distant and distracted.
- I knew my parents loved me, but they had a tough time saying it and showing it.
- One or both of my parents were emotionally unavailable.
- One or both of my parents would do anything to avoid having to deal with negative emotions of any kind.
- One or both of my parents wanted me to be happy all the time.
- One or both of my parents were warm, friendly, and loving.
- If my parents were upset with me, I was still treated with respect and dignity.
- One or both of my parents dealt with my negative emotions with love, patience, and support.
- My parents told me I was loved on a regular basis and showed it in actions.
- One or both of my parents validated my feelings and emotions.
- One or both of my parents were open and available and not afraid to show their emotions.

Exercise One: Self-Discovery

Write a brief statement capturing your childhood experiences and memories surrounding discipline. Then capture a belief or decision you made and finish with any *aha* moments or new insights.

Here are a few examples from parents who completed the exercise.

Skills for Expression

Impressions from Childhood

"My mother had a low tolerance for any negative emotions and would do anything to ensure we didn't have them. That meant we could control her with tantrums, outbursts and tears. It made for a very stressful childhood, and I didn't have much faith in my mom's ability to deal with life."

From Past to Present
"I decided that I would welcome every emotion in our home and focus on teaching my children how to express them and learn to deal with them in healthy ways."

Insight
"I do think I support the kids when they experience strong emotions, and they are getting better at bouncing back, but I don't really have the skills to express my emotions and I often become overwhelmed and explode."

Acknowledge Feelings
"I felt loved, valued, and respected in my family, and that lead to a fairly peaceful childhood. I feel confident in my ability to validate my children's emotions, listen to them, acknowledge what they are feeling and offer them the space to come up with solutions. My partner follows my lead; he wants to be engaged and involved, but has little experience with this type of interaction. He likes to make things better, but sees the value in what we are doing and is able to support me. I appreciate him for this."

Afraid to Shame
"Yelling, scolding, belittling were part of daily life, followed by insincere apologies. I loved my parents, but I was afraid of them and tried to distance myself from them. I wanted to make sure that when my children were adults, we had a very different relationship than I have with my parents. I never wanted them to feel humiliated or shamed by me or my reactions. I am recognizing that I can overlook issues that need to be dealt with because I am afraid I might start scolding the kids or they might interpret what I am saying as humiliating or shaming. I know I am going to have to start addressing issues head on and not worry so much about handling them perfectly."

Lacking Confidence

"My parents saved me from my bad choices or covered for me so I wouldn't get in trouble. It made me feel like they didn't think I could handle anything tough, and I doubted my ability to manage my own life. I wanted my kids to know their mom had faith in them and believed that they could learn from their mistakes and bounce back, but I keep interfering instead of allowing them to experience the negative consequences of their actions. I am sending mixed messages to the kids. I heard Vicki say once that you can't give your kids what you can't give yourself, and I think this is an example of what she meant. I have to have confidence in me before I can have confidence in them."

Modeling Level Headedness

"My parents thought it was important that I learn how to deal with disappointment, rejection and failure so I would learn to bounce back. They were both skilled in dealing with strong emotions and possessed a level-headedness that allowed all of us to have our feelings and emotions, no matter how strong, and wait until they subsided before any major decisions were made. They provided such a great model for dealing with emotions, and I am grateful for having them as an example. My partner and I try very hard to model for our children the way my parents did for my siblings and me. I am grateful that my partner is on board."

Unrealistic Expectations

"I was raised in a largely critical and rigid home. My parents had unrealistic expectations for their kids, but not themselves. They demanded unconditional respect but gave me little in return. I worried every day that I would be a disappointment to them. As a kid I swore I would never treat my own children the way my parents treated me. However, when it was my turn to be the boss, I did just that. Why? Because I had no role model for how to do it differently, which is exactly why I was attracted to my partner who was skilled at bringing out the best in people."

Inequitable Relationship

"I was raised in a loving, extended, Italian family. The adults in my life treated me with kindness and respect and made time for me. They listened to my stories of school and friends, were there to comfort me when I struggled and reminded me that when times were tough I could always count on them. I decided as a young person, and that decision solidified when I became a mother, that I would treat my children the way I was treated by the adults in my life. I struggle setting clear boundaries and following through if the kids get upset, which is exactly why I picked my partner, who embodies these qualities. I realized the kids have been playing us against each other, and instead of me learning from my partner how to do what he does, I depended on him to just do it. It made for an inequitable relationship and bad role modeling for the kids."

Emotional Health

"I felt loved, accepted, listened to and important to my parents. They were kind when I messed up and firm as well. They seemed to embody what true leadership in a family is, and I wanted to emulate that in my own family. The struggle began when I realized that my partner didn't have a real understanding of how important emotional health in young children is and is focused instead on their outward successes."

Exercise Two: A Vision for the Future

Using what you have discovered, write your vision for the future, including any action items you will incorporate into daily life with your family.

Here are some examples from clients to help illustrate this exercise.

Expressing Negative Emotions

"I am uncomfortable with negative emotions of any kind, and in a perfect world everyone would be happy all the time. This is not possible. I am ready to learn how to express my own negative emotions in a more positive way and to allow my kids to express their own without immediately thinking that if I was a good parent, they would be happy every minute of every day."

Support Emotional Expressions

"I have been letting myself and my kids express any emotion without any regard to how it affects other people. Instead of teaching the kids how to express with respect and consideration, we all just kind of vomit whatever emotion we are experiencing at the moment. I am ready to reconsider this approach and learn more about how to support the expression of emotions in a healthy way."

Exercise Three: Intersect, Parallel, Diverge

When you and your partner revisit this section, you will have a chance to share your experiences from Exercise One and Two and then move forward in creating a shared vision and a parenting plan to support that vision.

Based on your experiences, do you believe this is an area where you and your partner I (intersect), P (run parallel) or D (diverge)? Circle the best identifying category.

Conflict

There are many articles on the subject of fighting in front of the kids, and whether we should or should not. In my own life and my work as a parent coach, I have found that parents who had strong role models for conflict resolution can navigate this tricky area with ease and confidence. For others, conflict means a fight to the finish, rather than finding a middle ground in which to begin a dialogue. Think back to your own childhood experience and see if you can create a clear picture for how conflict was handled in your home when you were young. This will help you identify whether you are more interested in finding resolution or winning the battle, and it will help you evaluate your tolerance for different types of conflict.

There are many ways in which people respond to conflict; some prepare for battle, some run, some stay calm, some avoid, some give in and some might fall to the ground in a puddle of tears, believing they are unable to cope. All of these are solutions that we developed based on our experience as children.

Conflict can arise when parents have different views on important issues like finances, education, religion, friendships or in-laws. It can also arise over mundane things, like who takes out the trash, puts the kids to bed or helps with homework. Think about your own family, and if there were any areas that were particularly sensitive to one or both of your parents.

There is bound to be conflict between you and your partner as well as you and your children, and certainly between your children, so this is an area worth flushing out thoroughly to ensure you and your partner are able to support each other as you work toward peaceful resolutions.

Circle the statements that best capture your childhood experiences. Add your own if necessary.

- ◆ My parents dealt with conflict between them openly and honestly.
- ◆ My parents could easily agree to disagree.
- ◆ My parents avoided conflict at all costs.
- ◆ One or both of my parents tried to avoid conflict with me.
- ◆ My parents believed it was okay to argue in front of me.
- ◆ My parents never argued in front of me.
- ◆ My parents fought dirty and were often disrespectful of each other.
- ◆ My parents were able to disagree and maintain their respect for each other.
- ◆ One of my parents always gave in when there was a conflict.
- ◆ My parents and I always seemed to be in conflict.
- ◆ There wasn't much conflict between me and my parents because they were fair and reasonable.
- ◆ Conflict between family members was minimal.
- ◆ My parents had different views about important issues and would do or say anything to defend their position.

- ◆ Everything was a family problem. We all had input into solving issues big and small.
- ◆ My parents solved all the problems and stated what the resolution was and how we were to execute it.
- ◆ We might hurt each other in an argument, but we were quick to apologize and make amends.
- ◆ We were close so when there was conflict, we did what we could to resolve it quickly and respectfully.
- ◆ My whole childhood was one big conflict.

Exercise One: Self-Discovery

Write a brief statement capturing your childhood experiences and memories surrounding discipline. Then capture a belief or decision you made and finish with any *aha* moments or new insights.

Here are a few examples from parents who completed the exercise.

Normalizing Conflict

Impressions from Childhood

"My family fought loudly and unashamedly. But we had rules which included no hitting below the belt and getting personal. We could be yelling at each other and at the same time making cookies or braiding hair so conflict wasn't a scary thing for me."

From Past to Present

"I never really thought about doing anything differently as a parent. No matter the conflict, we always knew it was separate from us and always knew we were loved beyond measure."

Insight

"My partner avoids conflict and takes any harsh word or elevated tone personally. I feel as though I have to walk on eggshells, and it can be exhausting. I realize that his discomfort means the kids come to me and he misses out on an important part of their growth."

Healthy Conflict

"I never saw my folks argue! I believed that people who were happily married (or loved each other) didn't fight. I realize now that the tough work happened behind closed doors, and I missed out on learning some great life lessons that could serve me in my adult life. I often throw out *when you love someone, there is no need for conflict* when my partner wants to talk about something we don't agree on, which is like throwing gas on a fire. I can own that I have been making the conflict worse, not better, and it's time for me to learn healthy ways of dealing with conflict."

Avoiding Conflict

"We were a family of conflict avoiders. We would do anything to keep the atmosphere quiet and peaceful, however I always felt uneasy or like at any moment the rug would get pulled out and all the things we avoided would take over our home. I entered into relationships afraid of conflict. I sacrifice my beliefs and values to keep the peace, and it's important to me that people think I am easy to get along with. I never developed my voice and many problems go unresolved and fester. It is taking a toll on my physical and emotional health. I don't want this for myself or my kids, and I don't think my partner wants this either, but I have been unwilling to even explore this area of life with him."

Resentment and Betrayal

"Not only was there a lot of conflict in my home; it could last for days and days and turn into major resentments that would come out weeks later in an argument that was completely unrelated. I learned to avoid conflict, and even today, I don't trust most people and question their motives. It's not the conflict itself that is problematic for me; it's that I truly believe that my kids and my partner are keeping track of every one of my screw-ups and will throw it in my face later, so I go out of my way to find fault in other people. I had no ideas how this dynamic played out until I started to write."

Quiet and Polite

"My family gave the impression that there was never any conflict between us. Quiet voices, polite conversations, but underneath was a simmering pot of resentments and grudges. I wanted a home where conflict was seen as natural and not something to avoid, and I decided I would teach my kids how to talk calmly and rationally about difficult subjects. Of course, I had no experience with this, which is why I was attracted to my partner whose attitude includes *let's deal with it now until it's resolved*, which means addressing issues head on. As much as I liked the idea of dealing with conflict openly, I cringe every time we have to address a sensitive area where we are not in complete agreement."

Confused by Conflict

"Conflict was part of daily life in my home. Someone was always pissed about something. There was passive conflict and aggressive conflict. I learned to steer clear and to keep my thoughts to myself. I didn't consciously decide to avoid conflict, but I can see that I will do whatever I can to stop it before it starts and that makes for a very confusing parenting style for both my kids and my partner."

Picking Your Battles

"I came from a big family and we are all demonstrative, talked loudly and with our hands, which gives the impression to others that there is conflict. But the truth is, most conflict was dealt with quickly and respectfully. My parents had a very relaxed attitude about life, and they picked their battles carefully. I learned it was okay to disagree without making someone else wrong, and I definitely wanted to recreate this with my own kids. I can see that being with someone who has no experience with conflict resolution can increase the odds that there will be misunderstandings and tension."

Exercise Two: A Vision for the Future

Using what you have discovered, write your vision for the future, including any action items you will incorporate into daily life with your family.

Here are some examples from clients to help illustrate this exercise.

Generating a Solution

"When there is a disagreement, I would like all of us to be able to state our problem without shame or blame. I would like to incorporate a system that keeps the conversation calm and reasonable until we generate a solution that works for all of us. If someone gets upset and the yelling begins or someone shuts down, then we need to figure out how we are going to deal with emotions in the moment so we can come back and resolve the conflict."

Learning How to Listen

"I want each of us to feel heard. I will take the time to listen to the members of my family, practice validating their feelings, and executing their solutions. Even if I think I have a better idea, we need to practice generating solutions and listening to each other. There are too many hurt feelings and it will take some time to reestablish trust between us."

Exercise Three: Intersect, Parallel, Diverge

When you and your partner revisit this section, you will have a chance to share your experiences from Exercise One and Two and then move forward in creating a shared vision and a parenting plan to support that vision.

Based on your experiences, do you believe this is an area where you and your partner I (intersect), P (run parallel) or D (diverge)? Circle the best identifying category.

Independence

For those familiar with my work, you know that fostering independence in our children is a major focus of my programs and materials. I do believe that many challenges with our kids have more to do with our propensity to thwart their drive toward attaining independence than the need for a strategy to deal with some pesky behavior we find frustrating. Whether you are comfortable supporting your children's drive for independence, or nervous as they begin to strike out on their own more, how you handle this drive for independence will depend on your own experience as a child. Most of these questions are designed to bring you back to your younger, developmental years. They will help you identify the foundational principals of your beliefs. From there you can begin to write a story about independence in your own life and how that is translated into your parenting decisions with your own kids. You are looking for specific decisions you made, not generalities about the importance of independence.

Circle the statements that best capture your childhood experiences. Add your own if necessary.

- ◆ My parents had us participate in the household chores/ tasks.
- ◆ The household tasks were distributed evenly among all family members.
- ◆ My parents would bribe us and reward us for helping around the house.
- ◆ My parents did not think I could be trusted to remember details of my day.
- ◆ My parents trusted my ability to make decisions and manage my life.
- ◆ My parents trusted that I could handle the outcome of my choices and rebound from mistakes.
- ◆ My parents worked hard and went without as children and seemed to want an easier life for us as kids.
- ◆ My parents handled the big stuff like drugs, alcohol, sex, college, dating, driving, or our curfew with a calm confidence.
- ◆ My parents were so afraid of the "big" (see previous note) issues and tried to control and protect us from every risky mistake.
- ◆ My parents were absent. They called it benign neglect, but seriously, I could have spent a night in jail without them even noticing.
- ◆ We were encouraged to pick out our own clothes, make our lunch or breakfast, pick our own backpack or hair style.

+ My parents must have thought of us as nincompoops. We weren't even allowed to pack our own backpacks or take ownership of our schoolwork.
+ My parents were protective and restrictive of our music, movie choices, and televisions shows had to meet their stringent criteria.
+ My parents asked me to help brainstorm solutions to family problems.
+ My parents were afraid that if I didn't need them I wouldn't talk to them anymore.
+ My parents treated me like a "baby," and I felt resentful and embarrassed.
+ I loved having my parents do everything for me so I could have fun and do what I wanted.
+ My parents were the original helicopter parents.

Exercise One: Self-Discovery

Write a brief statement capturing your childhood experiences and memories surrounding discipline. Then capture a belief or decision you made and finish with any *aha* moments or new insights.

Here are a few examples from parents who completed the exercise.

Involved, Not Interfering

Impressions from Childhood

"My mother kept my clothes down low for easy access and encouraged me to choose what I would wear to school each day, and yet no matter what I picked, she made a comment on some aspect of my outfit. Either the socks were wrong, or the pants were too short or perhaps pigtails would look nice with that dress. It was independence with strings attached, which made me feel more like a puppet than an independent thinking young person."

From Past to Present

"I vowed that I would foster my children's budding independence at any cost, so I didn't become a hovering, overcontrolling, neurotic parent."

Insight

"After really thinking about what I wanted and what I am doing currently, I realize that my kids have been trying to tell me for a while that my hands-off approach leaves them feeling unsure or as if I don't care. My partner has tried to convince me that the kids need some form of feedback, and I have resisted him. I think it's time for a new conversation with everyone in the family, in order to find the balance of being involved without interfering."

Divide and Conquer

"I don't remember a time when I wasn't doing something to help my family. We had a divide and conquer attitude about life, and we depended on each other to help out when needed. My parents trusted me with things like getting up on time for school, packing my things for school and sports. I think they saw me as a responsible young person and treated me that way. I also remember them teaching me how to do stuff for myself, and I don't remember feeling pushed to grow up too fast. They did a nice job balancing this. I was determined to follow in their footsteps. I find I am tripped up when my kids act like they can't do something that I know they can. I don't seem to have the capacity to support them to take a leap forward, and instead I start shaming them and saying things like *sure you can, if you would just try.* More encouragement and gratitude on my part could easily solve this problem."

Responsibility and Independence

"My mom did everything for me. She was still waking me up and doing my laundry on demand when I was in high school. So in that way she treated me like a baby. But then she would let me stay on the computer as long as I wanted and stay over at my friend's house on school nights. I never really understood how independence and responsibility worked together, and I am still struggling with that balance. I knew that I wanted to offer my children the opportunity to take care of themselves and their belongings, but I wasn't sure how to go about it. Even though I knew that I didn't want to repeat my mother's parenting, I ended up doing the same things. I am perpetuating a vicious cycle. I need to step back and connect responsibility with independence."

Stickers and Rewards

"My parents came up with charts, stickers, rewards, punishments, anything to try and get me to help out around the house, but if I threw a big enough fit, they would just give me a lecture about how selfish I was or lazy I was, do the chore themselves and we would start the entire process all over again. I didn't believe that kids should have to help out around the house. There is enough time when they get older to take on all these responsibilities. Childhood is to be enjoyed. It is a time to make memories, not complete chores. My attitude was *if you want someone to do the housework, hire a maid.* I've known for some time that I was creating problems for my kids, myself and my partner, but I was too stubborn to admit that I was responsible for the mess we are in. I can't figure out how to motivate the kids to help, and I don't know what they could reasonably be doing at their ages. I can tell, even if they act like they want me to wait on them, they are losing confidence in themselves."

Suffocating Autonomy

"I wanted more independence and autonomy as a kid and decided I would give it to my kids when they were young, taking the time to teach them how to master skills that would help them throughout their lives. I think I sometimes go overboard and forget that they are still learning and that I could be more flexible when they oversleep or forget homework, or forget to put their laundry away. I realize this is why I jump all over my partner when she helps the kids. She is modeling flexibility, but

I immediately feel as though she is stunting their growth and working against me."

Maid, Not Mother

"My parents did everything for me, and I wanted to do the same thing for my kids. We also had help when I was growing up, and unfortunately I do not. Now I realize I am more like the maid than a mother, and I find I am resentful of the kids. I end up in this self-deprecating role, doing everything and being upset about it. When my partner tries to talk about it, I immediately get defensive, because I have not re-evaluated my initial goal of doing everything for my children."

Finding a Balance

"It can be tricky finding a balance between supporting independence and knowing kids can only handle so much. I can bounce from one extreme to the next if I'm not careful, and I think that confuses the kids and my partner. Because I am uncertain, I often snap at her if she questions a decision I have made in the moment. "

Embracing Growth

"I already see that independence for kids is an essential part of their self-esteem and confidence. My concern is that as they get older, I will want to hold them back because I am scared of the consequences, which would be far more significant than forgetting your science project in the third grade. This could easily be a point of contention with my partner, who feels strongly that allowing kids to make mistakes is necessary if they are to grow and learn."

Being the Boss

"I want to be the boss. I want to make the decisions. I don't care if the kids resist. It has been more important to me that I maintain my position as the expert in the family, and that has cost us all. There are daily power struggles between me and the kids, and my partner who is put off by my attitude has given up trying to talk to me about softening my approach."

Exercise Two: A Vision for the Future

Using what you have discovered, write your vision for the future, including any action items you will incorporate into daily life with your family.

Here are some examples from clients to help illustrate this exercise.

Teaching Necessary Skills

"To best support my children, I will learn to care less about a clean and tidy home and more about teaching them the necessary skills to build self-esteem and thrive on their own. The fact is, I need to develop a simple system that we can all stick to and that takes into account our crazy schedules. I am a go big or go home kind of gal, so starting small and gaining momentum is going to be key. My partner has a much more balanced approach to life and if I let go of my stubbornness he could be a big asset to all of us."

Provide Opportunities

"Instead of assuming that my kids can do whatever they put their minds to without any help from me, I will watch them and provide opportunities for them to practice with my help and encouragement before they become frustrated and discouraged and give up."

Exercise Three: Intersect, Parallel, Diverge

When you and your partner revisit this section, you will have a chance to share your experiences from Exercise One and Two and then move forward in creating a shared vision and a parenting plan to support that vision.

Based on your experiences, do you believe this is an area where you and your partner I (intersect), P (run parallel) or D (diverge)? Circle the best identifying category.

Education

Now more than ever, a child's education is a major focus in a parent's life. Some of the worry begins as early as preschool and follows the child until they graduate with a PhD in molecular biology. You would be hard-pressed to attend any social gathering and not hear the topic of education come up. Everyone has an opinion on the subject. Think back on your own experience. No doubt you have a meaning ascribed to the many conversations you had with your parents, or conversations you overheard your parents having about their feelings on the importance of education.

Circle the statements that best capture your childhood experiences. Add your own if necessary.

- ◆ Education was the number one priority for my parents.
- ◆ My parents were able to balance education with the other values in life.
- ◆ My parents were resentful of those who had completed a higher level of education and put more emphasis on hard work and grit.
- ◆ My parents dictated when and where and how much time we spent completing our homework.
- ◆ My parents were very involved in our homework and our school choices.
- ◆ My parents would meet with my teachers through high school and create learning plans and selected my courses.
- ◆ My parents valued education, but were mostly interested in my curiosity and supporting me as I developed a love of learning.
- ◆ My parents thought reading was for lazy people and always wanted me outside working on projects or developing a physical skill.
- ◆ Low grades were unacceptable, and I was grounded/punished/shamed if I ever had a grade lower than an A.
- ◆ My parents paid me for every A.
- ◆ My parents understood that grades were one measure of our learning. They focused more on the process of gathering information.

- ◆ I often felt as though it was more difficult to please my parents then it was to please my teachers.
- ◆ My parents left me to navigate my high school experience, but they were always available if I asked for help.
- ◆ My parents would support me by staying informed and connected with my school, but never overstepped any boundaries and let me dictate play.
- ◆ My parents would get so invested and excited about my school projects.
- ◆ My parents offered just enough support when it came to school projects/homework.
- ◆ I was always on my own when it came to school—sometimes it was perfect and sometimes I just missed assignments because I didn't care and I knew nobody else did either.
- ◆ I feel as though if my parents weren't leading the charge, I would have had a very different educational experience.
- ◆ I felt abandoned and barely graduated. I really would have appreciated some support.
- ◆ My parents would always drop off an assignment or write notes to my teachers if I was late handing in homework.
- ◆ My parents were always attacking my teachers. Any issue was never my fault.
- ◆ There was no choice. All of my siblings were expected to complete college and eventually go on for additional degrees.
- ◆ We had a choice. Whether we pursued additional education was up to each one of us.
- ◆ I could talk to my parents about what was happening in school.

Exercise One: Self-Discovery

Write a brief statement capturing your childhood experiences and memories surrounding education. Then capture a belief or decision you made and finish with any *aha* moments or new insights.

Here are a few examples from parents who completed the exercise.

Miscommunicated Values

Impressions from Childhood

"Homework, reading logs, portals, projects. The minute I got home, the conversation turned to school and continued for most of the night. It was clear that my parents put a premium on my success at school, and if I ever failed to deliver on the grades, I lost privileges until I brought my grades back up."

From Past to Present

"I did not want to put that type of pressure on my children and vowed to stay out of their school experience."

Insight

"As a result I think I have communicated to them that education is not important to me, as they don't take it seriously or put in much effort. I was so afraid of becoming my parents that I swung too far the other way, and when my partner tries to have a conversation with me, I get defensive and walk away. There is too much at stake for this to continue."

Pressure and Focus

"My parents were teachers. Doing well in school was a given. If I didn't do well, there were serious consequences. Even with a slight learning disability, my parents expected me to be at the top of my class. They pounded me every night with homework and even hired tutors to support my learning. I didn't realize that balance in life was also important. I pressure my children in the same way that my parents pressured me, even though I swore as a kid I wouldn't. You do what you know. This pressure and focus causes a rift between all of us. I can see how not taking the time to figure out what I believe about education and it's place in a child's life and then including my partner and my kids in conversations about education has left us in a very precarious situation."

Invested in Education

"My parents were teachers and they believed that as long as I invested in my education, it didn't matter what my grades were. They made it clear that I would have to take responsibility for my education, and they would be there to support me along the way. I felt empowered and carried my own pride around my schoolwork. If I made a mistake, I thought about a solution. I felt this was perfect and saw how it translated into other areas of my life. I work every day to create this same environment for my children. My partner grew up in a very different family. We both agreed that education was important to us and stopped the conversation there. We never identified how we would go about supporting our children, and we fight constantly. I think we are on the same page, but all of the fighting gets in the way of us discovering that."

Loving Life

"My parents both had high-powered jobs and expected their kids to not only go to college, but graduate school as well. They really believed that my happiness in life depended on this, because it would ensure I landed a high paying job. I remember even today, shaking my head and thinking, *If this is happiness, I would rather be miserable.* I am the black sheep of the family. I graduated with a master's in anthropology, and my partner and I have started a family farm. We barely get by and work very hard to make ends meet, but I am happier than I have ever been. I don't want my kids to feel any type of pressure and do not want them correlating a degree from school with happiness in life. I believe being happy is much more important than getting good grades or a competitive salary. I want my kids to be good people, work hard, play hard and love their lives. Whatever direction that takes them, they have my support."

Exercise Two: A Vision for the Future

Using what you have discovered write your vision for the future, including any action items you will incorporate into daily life with your family. Here are some examples.

Creating Curious Consumers

"I want my children to enjoy the process of learning and to be curious consumers of information. I don't want to focus on grades. I will change my focus and ask a specific list of questions that engages their minds and help them identify how they learn best."

Education in a Nutshell

"I believe that in order to support yourself and your family, you must have a college degree. My children's quality of life as adults will directly correlate to the quality of their education. We will have strict guidelines about homework and schoolwork, and when their responsibilities are met, they will then be able to play."

Exercise Three: Intersect, Parallel, Diverge

When you and your partner revisit this section, you will have a chance to share your experiences from Exercise One and Two and then move forward in creating a shared vision and a parenting plan to support that vision.

Based on your experiences, do you believe this is an area where you and your partner I (intersect), P (run parallel) or D (diverge)? Circle the best identifying category.

The Topic of Sexuality

It might appear delinquent if I did not include a section on sexuality here, but the truth is parents are just now beginning to recognize the necessity in talking with their children of both genders about sex, sexuality, pornography, consent, the rape culture and so much more. We do as parents bring our experiences and beliefs to the table when parenting our kids around this topic, and this topic would be an entire book itself. I have included a list of resources on my website (www.vickihoefle.com) for you as a way to introduce you to this delicate subject, and it is my sincere hope that you will dive in with bravery and an open mind and create a value statement with your partner. Our children need us to know what they are faced with each day, and they need us to be there to help them navigate through all the misinformation, peer and social pressure and build confidence so they can make informed decisions and keep themselves safe from harm as they grow and mature.

Part II
Working Together

7

Creating Your Partnership

Before your child was born, you made the time to create the perfect infant room, you decided what kind of diapers you would use, if you would breast or bottle feed, if you would make your own baby food or not. Maybe by now you have planned memorable birthday parties and vacations or decided you would create unstructured time and let creativity flow. You could be living with a middle-schooler and have boxes of saved science and art projects and countless pictures documenting every phase of your child's life. The goal of this book is to help you create a plan with your partner and understand the value of investing the time that will ensure you raise the kind of people who can fulfill their own potential, find happiness in daily life and remain close and connected to you and the other members of your family, no matter what the circumstances may be. In other words, my aim is to support you as you gather everything you need to launch your kids without ejecting your spouse in the process.

You have taken your trusty spotlight and with a healthy dose of courage explored three aspects of family life; the relationships between family members, the day to day operations of a busy family and the lifestyle choices that oftentimes define a family. It's likely you uncovered lost memories, reclaimed significant experiences, and gained new insights into your parenting, and you have begun to see some patterns emerge. Patterns that until now were guiding your parenting decisions without you even realizing it. Identifying these patterns can help. Perhaps these patterns revealed areas where you thought you would remain calm, cool and collected but instead resulted in your acting like an out of control three year old, hopped up on sugar, or situations that have the potential to send any parent into orbit and you navigate them with grace, respect and confidence. Not knowing how we will react in any given situation can be unnerving for us parents. Not knowing how our partner will respond adds to that anxiety, and knowing that the two of you don't agree on how to handle a situation with your kids further adds unnecessary tension. When we feel caught off guard, or believe we are losing control of a situation, it's easy to become reactionary and begin to parent from a place of fear rather than one of confidence. As our confidence erodes and we begin to second guess ourselves, we look for answers in all the usual places: books, blogs and friends. Identifying patterns in our behavior can help us gain confidence and make it easier for us to open up to our partner in the hopes of coming together in the best interest of our kids.

Once you discover answers to some of the most confusing and frustrating parenting challenges, working together with your partner will be so much easier. Now that you know that all those seemingly unrelated responses to everyday parenting challenges can be traced back to your childhood experiences, the meaning you ascribed to them and the decisions you made based on the meaning, you are shining a light on the source of the solution. In other words, your past is influencing your present and in this particular case your parenting life.

Instead of trying to change your past (which is impossible), you have the opportunity now to use all your new insight to create a clear path that will offer your children the best shot at living a healthy, happy and productive life and ensure that you and your partner maintain a respectful, supportive and exciting co-parenting life together for years to come. In other words, no one is getting ejected.

All of our experiences are connected. Our lives are a tapestry of beliefs that inform us and guide our every decision. Nowhere is this more apparent than in our roles as parents, and it is here that we can use this information to break through outdated, limiting beliefs and habits and create new, healthy, expansive beliefs and habits that allow us to work with our partner in deeper and more meaningful ways.

The hard work is over. You have learned about your own childhood experiences and you have learned about your spouse and their experience. You have found places of intersection, places where there is overlap and places that, once challenging, now hold the potential to bring you closer together as a couple and a parenting team. It's time to put all the pieces together, and with the patience and courage you have cultivated by completing the previous exercises and the dedication and commitment to working together with your partner as a team to provide the most consistent and stable environment in which to raise your children, you are ready to forge ahead.

At the end of this chapter, you will have everything you need to create a thoughtful, intentionally designed, deeply personal parenting plan to guide you on this magical and sometimes mysterious journey we call parenting.

Working Together

1. Before you share your memories and insight with your partner and begin working on your shared vision and parenting plan together, create a space that is safe, where you have time, you are both focused, and all of your devices are not only turned off, but they are out of the room. You would be surprised at how many sessions have been sabotaged because of a small vibration from a device that will take you immediately out of the experience and place you smack dab into something that isn't nearly as important as this moment.

2. Commit a certain amount of time to work on your parenting plan together and anchor the experience by celebrating

when you have finished one session. Even if you have hit a few rocky moments, it's still worth focusing on how committed you are to your kids and to your marriage, and that deserves a moment of acknowledgement and celebration.

3. Go slowly and thoughtfully. It isn't a race. It's better to focus on one particular area and create a plan you are willing to try for a week or two than it is to try and make changes to multiple areas at one time. Slow and steady wins the race.

4. You are not here to change each other, but to learn about yourselves and each other. Do not spend time trying to convince your partner that your way is the best way; to talk them out of their own ideas; to become their personal therapist so they can heal from childhood wounds; to criticize, judge, evaluate or anything else that might create unnecessary tension, stress, distance, mistrust or disconnection. Listening and remaining attentive are all that is required.

5. Start each and every interaction with an appreciation. In my experience, every interaction, especially those that touch the sensitive areas of our lives, are much more successful when we begin with an appreciation. In fact, they can be so powerful that any time you begin to feel distance growing between you and your partner or feel your defenses being activated, taking the time to share an appreciation will quickly re-center you both and allow you to proceed forward in an atmosphere of unity, camaraderie and trust.

Examples of Appreciations

♦ I appreciate you setting time aside today to explore your childhood experiences so we can co-parent in a more rewarding and satisfying way.

♦ I appreciate your willingness to explore this work and its potential to bring us closer as a couple and as parenting partners.

♦ I appreciate your willingness to take a look at your belief about women and their roles as mothers, and I understand the courage that it takes to go back to your childhood and explore the decisions you may have made.

◆ I appreciate how sensitive you are when I talk about some of my difficult childhood experiences.

◆ I appreciate that sharing doesn't come naturally, and yet because of your commitment to the kids and our marriage, you are willing to jump in with both feet.

◆ Thank you for showing up.

◆ Thanks for letting me say everything I needed to say.

◆ I appreciate how patient you are.

◆ I appreciate the way you focus in on what I am saying when I share something from my past.

Although we think we came together with our partner with shared ideas about child-rearing, it's clear by now that those intersections were only surface deep. Right below the surface are murky waters filled with unforeseen forces that will take hold and pull one or both of you down until it is nearly impossible to find your footing and come together to parent as a team rather than opponents. Appreciations are your lifelines, so use them generously.

6. Be sure not to confuse your parenting style with the decisions you made about how you would parent as a result of your early memories. We generally think of parenting styles in terms of authoritarian, permissive or democratic, but in this instance I am expanding the definition to include your natural temperaments and rhythms. For instance, I am a night owl and function best after 7:30 p.m., while my partner is a morning lark and is at his best at 5:00 a.m. We had to accommodate each other's styles rather than try and force the other to change. As it turns out, our children ranged from night owls to morning larks, and it made it quite easy for us to support them after we found ways to support each other. One daughter did homework at 5:00 a.m. and another at 10:00 p.m. Both did well in school because we used their natural rhythms when making our parenting decisions. This

might not have been the case, had we not taken the time to learn and then support each other and extend that courtesy to our kids. You might be an extrovert and your partner an introvert, and you will do better to support your partner's natural temperament, rather than try to change it or criticize it. One of you might have a very low threshold for noise while the other enjoys loud and raucous music. The point is, be sure you are not trying to change the person you are married to. You'd be better off spending your time learning how to cooperate with someone who sees and moves through the world differently. I have never found trying to change someone to be a fruitful endeavor.

7. When strong emotions arise, and they will, stop. Tell your partner that you are having a strong emotional response to what you are saying or what you are hearing. Take responsibility for this. Breathe, stay calm, allow the feelings to come up and then watch them drift away like clouds. If you begin to talk about your feelings at this point, you will get sidetracked, and before you know it, you will close up the book and toss it out with yesterday's garbage. This is tough work, and as tough work goes, it takes commitment, a safe environment, honesty, trust and above all else, the ability to take responsibility for what is yours, and that includes any anger, hostility, sadness, guilt, resentment, confusion, joy, exuberance, insight or wisdom. When we take responsibility for our own feelings, emotions and experiences, we are capable of addressing sensitive issues that might otherwise derail the entire process. If you or your partner begin to anchor the feeling, giving it attention and energy so that it lasts longer than is natural (no more than fifteen to thirty seconds), take a break. These are often pivotal moments in the process. They can be and often are cathartic, and if you have the courage to stay with it, you will be rewarded with a new clarity to a situation that until now has seemed confusing and frustrating. Imagine the elation you will feel when this happens.

8. When you find an area where you are at odds—or so it may seem on the surface—it's time to use questions to flush out differences and find where your ideas might in fact intersect. I encourage you to record any questions you generate that allow you to move the process forward, as they will work in any number of situations and once you become adept at them, you will notice how easily you incorporate them into your daily life. Let me say now that successful co-parenting includes mastering the art of appreciative inquiry (asking questions), and once you do, you will see the relationship with not only your spouse but your children improve immensely. When you begin to feel stuck or that things are taking a turn for the worse, it's almost always because we have abandoned appreciative inquiry and replaced it with judgment, criticism, directives, orders, nagging or some other unsavory way of communicating.

Examples of Appreciative Inquiry

- ◆ What is possible if we explore other options together?
- ◆ What will life be like if we make this change?
- ◆ Who benefits if we find a mutually satisfying solution?
- ◆ What will it take to find common ground in this situation?
- ◆ How will we make this happen?
- ◆ What are we willing to give up in order to get what we want?
- ◆ What possibilities exist that we haven't considered?
- ◆ What will it take for us to come to an agreement?
- ◆ What will we sacrifice if we do not change how we respond?
- ◆ Who is most at risk if we continue communicating in our current style?
- ◆ What is the best possible outcome for everyone?

Simply put, appreciative inquiry creates space for possibilities to be considered. Statements tend to support our positions or opinions and often activate the listener who then makes a statement about their position. If you find yourself on the hamster wheel of *yeah buts*, it's time for a strong question to get you moving forward again.

9. If you don't have a strong feeling about an area of life you are exploring—say, for example, manners—then be clear that you will defer to your partner's ideas. If you find later that the outcome is causing your spouse, your child or you stress in any way, revisit the issue. Be sure to come to the table with some ideas on how you might both rethink your approach going forward.

Creating Your Plan

The parenting plan you are about to create with your partner will support both of you as individuals and as a co-parenting team, as well as your children, who have their own unique ways of moving through the world, and your family as a whole. At the end of this chapter, you will have created a thoughtful, intentionally designed, deeply personal parenting plan to guide you on this magical and sometimes mysterious journey we call parenting.

In my consultation work with parents, I encourage them to create a visual representation of their plan to use as a guide in helping them choose an area to start their work and a way to track their progress with specific milestones to ensure they make progress and acknowledge improvement. Some parents use a journal to document their journey; others use a visual road map to help them identify the steps they will take to reach their ultimate goal. I myself found that putting very large yellow sticky notes on the wall of my bedroom, with small, reachable weekly goals, along with steps I was willing to take, kept me focused on what was most important to me and held me accountable without making me feel bad when I slipped back to my old ways.

Exercise Creates Insight

Personally, if I had known how much smoother life could be for my partner and me, not to mention our children, I would have done this exercise weeks before I finally found time for it. The insights, *aha* moments, the compassion and the hope it gave us cannot be described with words. Now, whenever one of us overreacts, we know that there is a story that is holding the other parent hostage, and if we can ride the storm and get to the other side, we can sit down, sort through it and come to a clear understanding about what is right for us as a parenting team and what is right for our child. It is not only liberating to know that you have a tool to help guide you; it is life changing.

Step One: Share Your Memories

Read the observations you made about your family life at the end of Exercise One and your vision for the future from Exercise Two to your spouse, and if it feels right, share more of your early impressions of life in your family. Once you feel satisfied that your partner has a clear understanding of your childhood and the decisions you made based on your experiences, allow your partner to do the same. Remember, by understanding your partner's views, beliefs and perspectives based on their childhood experiences, there is no longer any reason to spend time trying to convince each other someone is wrong and must change. Be careful that you don't slip into old communication patterns that include commenting on what your partner is saying, editorializing, correcting or disagreeing with your partner's memories, observations or decisions. Instead focus all your innate talent and the love you have for each other in stating your mutual goal and then finding ways to meet those goals.

Step Two: Identifying the Category

After you have shared, continue to Exercise Three. This exercise will help you identify if this is an area where you intersect, run parallel or diverge. Circle the appropriate category and make a note so you can return later to develop a new parenting plan with your partner or begin your work immediately if it feels right.

Intersect

Intersections are areas in which you both hold a shared value, belief and goal. Your experiences may have been similar, or they could have been completely different, but the decisions you made based on those early memories align. Similarly, your insights might suggest that you both see an opportunity for improvement and Exercise Two confirms that you have a shared vision for the future and that you want the same thing for the same reasons.

Run Parallel

Parallels are areas in which some of your ideas, preferences and goals are similar in nature, but you aren't in full agreement about how to execute your goals. There are examples throughout the book of parents recognizing those parallel areas if you aren't sure. The story of parents who both wanted to support independence in their children, but had very different definitions of what independence meant, is one example.

Parallels can look harmless on the surface at first glance, but there is a chance that if you dive into this area of life and try and make a decision with your partner, it might ignite something in you, and suddenly you and your parenting partner are at odds over something that seemed insignificant moments before. They can also become default areas of parenting and can cause quite a bit of confusion for the kids as their parents grapple with changing strategies as well as revolving responses to challenges that arise.

Diverge

You want one thing and your partner wants the opposite, and you are certain your ideas, values, perspective and attitudes diverge, as does your vision for the future. It will be clear in what areas you and your partner have diverging ideas as you share your stories and your vision for the future. Don't panic. We are bound to find areas where we see things very differently, but that doesn't mean we can't find a way to work together going forward. You have a choice in this moment. Imagine that you are each holding one end of a rope. You could continue trying to drag your partner over to your side, or you can admit that if you both walked your hands toward the center, you might find common ground and a way to create a plan that takes into account both of your ideas, values and perspectives. And this is possible if you have taken the time to learn about your partner's childhood experiences and how he/she came to make some of the many parenting decisions each day. Compassion and understanding go a long way in resolving diverging perspectives, values and goals.

It is difficult to show our vulnerabilities, even to our life partner, and here more than ever, you will both have to walk gently toward each other rather than stand firm on defending your positions or pointing out where the other is wrong. If you cannot come to some understanding, then not only will your marriage suffer; your children will as well. Hence the name of the book: if you want to successfully launch your kids without ejecting your spouse, you will have to be gentle with yourself and with each other. It's time to make a decision. Do you put your ego aside, ask for support from your spouse, listen to constructive feedback and move forward toward the creation of a co-parenting plan, or do you throw in the towel and call it quits. (Imagine your kids are watching you at this very moment—who do you want them to see?)

Step Three: Getting Started

I recommend you start your work with an area of life where you and your partner have intersecting ideas, values and perspectives or are currently navigating well. Maybe bedtimes are seamless, or you agree on giving the kids an allowance, or on how much help you will give the kids with homework. The goal is to get you working together consciously and thoughtfully as a way to build your own partnership, model for the kids what true co-parenting looks like and to bring about slow, progressive change in your family if that is what you are hoping to do.

Once you create plans for the areas in which your ideas and views intersect, move on to the areas in which your ideas and views run parallel. Finally, embrace those areas where you are fairly certain your ideas, views, perspectives, attitudes and even beliefs diverge, and give it a go. Writing a plan in an area where you diverge requires a few extra steps (four to be exact) to ensure your success.

When You Diverge

1. Once you have shared your memories and the decisions you made in Steps One and Two, stop and give an appreciation. Yes, an appreciation. This is going to be sensitive work, so why not ensure that you start out with a loving heart and an open mind? Here are a few suggestions to get you started, although by now, it's probably feeling a bit like second nature.

   I appreciate how challenging it must be to have the kids show you disrespect in the form of their words or behaviors, especially knowing how hurtful it was when your own parents treated you with disrespect, but demanded you respect them. Is there a way for us to redefine what the word means and three ways in which we can help our kids learn to show themselves and others respect? I know you do not want to do to our kids, what your parents did to you. I am here to try as many things as we need to in order to find a solution.

   I appreciate how much you want our kids to go to college, because you never got the chance and you decided that being involved in every aspect of their education was the way to ensure that, and yet you are open to finding a balance and allowing our kids to take a more active role in designing their future with us as co-pilots, not the drivers.

   I appreciate that manners were hammered into your head as a kid and that you spent time with the kind of people that would have looked down on your family if you didn't demonstrate them. I know it's tough not to correct the kids,

*and I will do whatever I can to help promote manners with-
out risking the relationship we have with our children.*

2. Make a promise not to become the therapist or to try and change the way your partner looks at the situation. They do not need to be fixed or to change the way they interpret their childhood experiences. They are who they are. Your goal is to come together as partners, parenting together, and decide what is in your child's best interest. There is no need to talk it out. If you wish to do that, schedule another time to dive into those dark corners or hire a therapist to help you.
3. Go slowly. A willingness to try something new with the commitment to actually respond differently is enough to get the change process in motion. Keep things simple by changing one thing at a time.
4. When you feel yourself sliding down a slippery slope of blame, shame, criticism or judgment, stop and return to appreciative inquiry, outlined earlier in this chapter.

Step Four—Your Shared Vision for the Future

Write your shared vision. Here are a few more to get your juices flowing.

Mealtime Connection
"As a couple, we understand the value of having family dinners together and will do our best to create a calm, relaxed atmosphere where the focus is on reconnecting and sharing our day and will introduce fundamental manners in a gentle and consistent way."

Opportunities for Learning
"As parenting partners we agree that our children's education is a top priority and that we could easily become too involved in their school life if we aren't careful. We will work together to help our children develop a love of learning, while accepting that they will experience upsets and failures from time to time, and will consider these opportunities for learning."

Parenting as Partners

"We want our kids to look back on their childhood and say, 'Our parents worked together equally in the raising of their children. They were a true partnership. They had deep respect for each other and their children and demonstrated this through their words, attitudes, and actions. We were included in decision making and other important aspects of family life, and they made sure that they were available when we needed them.'"

Step Five—Design Your Plan

Whether your kids are still in utero or hitting the tween years, start where you are to create a meaningful plan that you can execute the majority of the time. Do not complicate it. Keep it simple. Know where the boundaries are to hold the plan firm, and know where you can be flexible, as life is dynamic, and if your plan is too rigid, it will break.

Writing down a few details and identifying things that trip you up will ensure you experience success, and with it a new freedom and exhilaration that comes from working with your partner, rather than against him or her.

Examples are listed at the end of the chapter.

Step Six—Implement Your Plan

Give yourself a few weeks to institute your new parenting plan so that your family isn't thrown into complete chaos. There is no rush. Small, subtle shifts in your words, actions and attitude, along with a commitment to follow-through on your plan, is enough to bring about substantial and lasting change. Within a few days you will begin to notice a new and more cooperative language emerge between you and your partner, and this will set the tone for all your other encounters. And it's possible that you will hit a few speed bumps along the way, so use appreciative inquiry to keep the conversation moving forward in a positive direction. The goal is to work together, not to revamp your entire family in two weeks. Besides, most families

I have worked with don't need an overhaul, just a few minor adjustments.

Keys to Success

Once you agree to a new plan to deal with some area of life with the kids, keep these tips in mind to ensure ongoing success.

1. Avoid criticizing your partner, especially in front of the kids. It's one thing to disagree, *I understand, but I am not sure I agree. Can we discuss this before we make a decision?* and another to openly criticize, *You are talking too much. Try listening for a change and maybe you will understand what is really going on here.* Everyone loses when criticism is at play.

2. If you know you are about to say something you will regret later, walk away. You are not giving up and you are not giving in. You are maintaining your own dignity and respect and extending it to your partner and children. Everyone wins. If you do open your mouth, apologize when you have recovered and be sure your children see and hear you do it. You are modeling the kind of behavior you want them to exhibit, so don't shy away from your mistakes. Own these mistakes and move on.

3. Before you find fault in your partner, ask yourself what you could do to make things better. It's always easier to blame and complain about our partner, rather than looking in the mirror and owning our own part in a problem or misunderstanding.

4. Cultivate a grateful attitude. When you do, you begin to notice the best in yourself, your partner, your kids, heck everyone and everything. As a result you are slower to anger, quicker to forgive, and you model for your kids the kind of spouse and partner you hope them to grow into.

5. Create a living legacy for your kids that is based on a strong, respectful, and loving partnership with their other parent. When you do, you ensure that your own children will look for individuals who model the same qualities and character traits that you are working hard to model and instill in your children.

Example of Intersecting Ideas of Bedtimes

Art and Maggie

Art and Maggie both have strong and fond memories of bedtime. When they shared memories from Part I, they realized that their bedtimes were reasonable for their ages, and their parents did not waiver just because something fun might be going on at their homes. Maggie shared a story to illustrate. "Whenever I think of bedtime, I get this warm, gooey feeling in my belly. It wasn't until I looked deeper and explored what bedtime really meant in my home, that I was able to articulate exactly why I had that feeling. I remember once, we had people at our home for a big barbecue. It was getting close to bedtime and I was about to start begging to stay up and continue in the fun, when my dad came over, took my hand and said, 'I need some time with just you!' At that moment, I would have followed him anywhere. It turns out he was taking me to bed, but I didn't care. Just as I had a scheduled bedtime, we had a consistent ritual, and when I saw that my dad was willing to leave the party and spend that special time with me, I didn't resist at all. My parents laid the groundwork for peaceful bedtimes, and that is what I want to do with my kids."

Art has a similar story, which includes a simple bedtime routine, a final connection with his parents before he and his much adored older brother were left to talk quietly in bed before Art nodded off to sleep. He too wants to recreate this experience with his kids.

Based on their observations and the decisions they identified in Part II, they were able to write their shared vision for bedtime, which includes, most importantly, that their children experience a sense of connection, continuity and consistency. With this shared vision, they can now create a simple routine that ensures a peaceful bedtime for their kids.

Here are just a few questions that Art and Maggie will want to consider as they formalize the details of their potential plan.

◆ What is a reasonable bedtime for the age and temperament of the child?

- How long will the ritual last?
- Will you lay down with the child, even if it isn't part of your plan, if they ask you?
- What is likely to trip you up, and how will you support each other through these moments?
- What will you do if the child comes out of their room repeatedly?
- Is there ever any reason to extend bedtime if you are at home?
- Does bedtime and ritual happen when you are away from home?
- Do you ever modify the ritual? Although you might not think this is important, imagine a scenario in which you both visit friends, you are having a lovely visit by the outside fire and it's time for one of you to leave to tend to the kids. Is there any room for hurt feelings or resentment to grow? Or, perhaps one of you has been with the kids all day and you are feeling depleted and would love a bedtime break, but your partner says they need to finish up an important email and get it off before the end of the evening. My partner and I came up with a code to help us get through these moments, which happened more than you might think. Instead of playing rock, paper, scissors, we used a one to five finger rating system to indicate our ability to successfully deploy our bedtime plan. One finger meant you could not get behind it, and five fingers meant you were on top of your game and ready to go.

Once they got clear on the details, they were ready to design a simple plan that would ensure their daughter was blessed with the same fond memories of bedtime that both Art and Maggie had when they were children.

"We both remember feeling very settled as kids and being given the opportunity to say good night slowly, rather than being rushed. Our goal is to have our daughter associate bedtime with these same feelings. Our daughter is two years old and we have decided that 8:30 p.m. is a reasonable bedtime if she has taken an afternoon nap, and 7:00 p.m. if she missed the nap. This ensures that she does not hit critical mass, and we can enjoy our time together before we put her to bed. Our ritual includes saying good night to the things we love, like our dog, pictures of nanna and pops, a special bunny, one picture book, a last snuggle and kiss and then lights out. We know it won't be without its challenges, but now that we have a plan, we feel better prepared to deal with any pushback she might give us and hold firm to a plan we believe in.

As we talked, we recognized that part of the reason our parents created a bedtime ritual was to ensure they would have time for themselves and their adult relationship after their kids were in bed. This explains why both of our parents were involved in the ritual. If you know you are going to have time once the kids go to bed, then you can work together instead of the divide and conquer mind-set so many parents adopt once they have kids. We could suddenly see how this simple routine could help keep all of us healthy and create lasting, positive habits."

Oftentimes, parents think it's enough to have a shared experience to use as a guide, but remember, your kids did not grow up in your home. You are working from scratch and if you want to ensure that your kids have the same fond memories around bedtime as you do of your childhood, you will have to give your new plan, time, thought, preparation, planning and then be patient. And there are always those pesky trip-ups to consider so be sure and flush those out before they make an unseemly entrance.

Parallel Ideas of Independence

Charles and Peter

"Charles and I identified a parallel area when we read about independence. Initially we thought we would be on the same page, but after a bit of discussion we quickly realized we could easily misunderstand the other if we hadn't taken the time to flush out what the word independence means to each of us. Turns out my definition of independence is that kids are free to explore and learn without a lot of parental supervision or direction. Charles's definition is that kids should learn how to take care of themselves and help out around the house. So although we both want to foster independence, we have to redefine what that word means for us now as parents and how we can mesh our two ideas together. For instance, I want to put out the paints and paper and let the kids explore their artistic side, and Charles wants to ensure the kids put all their supplies away when they are done. I would have naturally set things up and then cleaned up after the kids. Very quickly we understood why we would fight anytime I suggested an art or cooking project, and why I got so annoyed when Charles was focused on the damn cleanup process. Now we both know it's possible to support independence in any number of ways and can support each other in our goal of fostering independence and self-reliance, as well as cooperation in our kids.

We didn't stop with our shared vision. We know we can't really be trusted with just an 'idea' for a plan. We took the time to map it out and write it up and put it up on a wall so we could refer to it until it became a habit. As a result, when one of us started sliding into our old ways, we would take the hand of our beloved, walk into the bedroom and just say, 'Read this,' and whoever was steering off course would immediately come back to center. We would end up hugging and feeling so elated that we were actually working for our kids instead of for ourselves."

Diverging Ideas of Respect

Josh and Mary

"Josh and I know that we define respect in very different ways. I am a free spirit by nature, and I don't take things personally. My entire family growing up spent time showing respect rather than talking about it. Josh on the other hand came from a highly critical family who demanded their children show them respect in spite of the fact that they showed their children almost none. We knew this was an area of conflict for us, but we could never figure out how to move past it. When one of the kids was even slightly disrespectful to Josh, he would lash out at them and then demand they apologize and lecture them about respect. My responses ranged from rolling my eyes or spitting out, 'It's no big deal,' or 'They didn't mean it,' or when I was really pissed, I'd hit below the belt and yell, 'Is your ego so fragile that you can't let a little childish disrespect go?' Each time this happens we dig deeper into defending our positions. Obviously there is no respect in any of these interactions."

In order for Josh and Mary to move toward each other, they will have to decide what one thing they will both do differently in order to come closer to a solution that works for everyone. It might be as simple as Mary saying to one of the kids, "I can see you are upset, is there another way you could say that?" Having a partner who understands and affirms your beliefs, whether they agree with them or not, is enough to ease the tension in the moment and bring you back in alignment with what is most important, and in this case, it is modeling and supporting respectful relationships.

Josh shared the following: "As soon as Mary understood where this need for respect came from, she became my ally rather than my adversary. Whenever she heard the kids use disrespectful language or a disrespectful tone with anyone, she quickly helped them practice a different way of expressing themselves that wasn't at the cost of anyone else. I felt supported, validated and loved. I was less triggered by the kids knowing that Mary had my back. Within a few short weeks, I was less sensitive and focused my attention on showing rather than demanding respect, and the kids responded in kind. We are a happier and far more respectful family, and it was as simple as coming to terms with my own belief system, working with my partner and then executing our plan for a healthy and loving family. Success all around."

Tying it Together

Launching our children without ejecting our spouse was the phrase that best captured my clients' wishes when we discussed parenting and their desire to raise children in an atmosphere of love and respect. With few resources to assist them in their quest to co-parent cooperatively, along with their mission to raise awesome kids who had fond memories of their childhood, I felt compelled to jump in and share my ideas on what it takes to co-parent successfully. Over the last twenty-five years I have been coaching parents on how to come together as a parent team and work together in the best interest of their kids. This requires that they both accept the fact that they each bring their own ideas, values and perspectives on how to best raise great kids. This coaching includes specific tools to help parents collaborate and incorporate each of their experiences, ideas and goals into a cohesive plan for raising their children from birth to young adulthood (and beyond). This book is the result of that work. My hope is that more and more parenting partners will find ways to work together in the best interest of their children. My hope is that more parenting partners will become role models for their kids on how to work cooperatively and collaboratively with their own partners, as well as everyone else they find themselves in relationship with, when the time comes. Enjoy the journey, forgive yourself and your partner often and quickly, and remind yourself again and again that your children are watching and learning from you. I urge you to show them how loving partnerships really work.

8

Stories from the Trenches

Intersecting

Eva and Avery: Sibling Relationships

"We found our first intersection when we realized that the relationships we had with our siblings wasn't the kind of relationship we wanted our kids to have with each other. What we quickly realized was that we were trying to force our kids to like each other. We were saying things like 'You are so lucky to have a sister who. . .,' and we would get eye rolls from both kids or they would respond with 'I hate her.' This would usually activate one of us, and we responded by yelling at the kids, which would activate the other parent, and before you could count to three, we were yelling at each other. It was a cycle we couldn't seem to break. We knew what we wanted but we didn't know how to get there, which makes sense since neither of us knows how to connect with our own brothers and sisters. We used our desire to help foster strong relationships between the kids along with our own experiences with our adult friends to come up with a short list of ways we could help the kids learn to enjoy each other's company instead of trying to force them into being best friends. One strategy that we incorporated into our plan that has worked exceptionally well has been our use of appreciations with the kids and with each other. Initially, we both felt awkward, but over time, our confidence grew, and with it our use of them at random times. Lo and behold, the kids started giving us appreciations and then each other. That alone is transforming their relationship. Committing to this one strategy inspired us, and now we have an ongoing list of things we can do to foster all of the relationships in our home. Knowing that we were on the same page was a bit of a thrill for us. It deepened our conversations, and finding this initial intersection ignited a fire in both of us. Now we look forward to finding others and working together in the best interest of our kids."

Run Parallel

Agnes and George: Parenting Roles

"My mother was wishy-washy, inconsistent and preoccupied throughout my childhood. It was nearly impossible to guess how she would respond in a situation. Her reactions depended upon who was around, how she was feeling and if she was upset with me or one of my siblings. I felt uneasy and struggled with trusting her. I didn't want to be anything like her as a parent. I wanted my kids to feel confident that I knew what I was doing." George had a very different memory of his mother, "My mother was a bulldog. She dealt with things head on which means sometimes there was fall out, but all in all, she parented with confidence and I always felt safe because of your tenacious and dedicated attitude toward us kids. I wanted my partner to have these same qualities and to trust herself when she made parenting decisions."

After sharing their memories, the decisions they made and their *aha* moments with each other, George and Agnes were ready to create a shared vision. "It took us a while to get clear on what we really wanted, but it boiled down to this: children need to know that their parents know what they are doing, believe the decisions they make are in the best interest of their children, and are open to changing their minds and will when necessary.

It was important for us to identify what would trip us up, and we developed a plan to support each other until these didn't feel like landmines ready to blow us out of the water if we landed on one. That simple exercise and a plan for supporting each other has changed everything in our home. With just a subtle look or touch, we have the capacity to refocus our attention on our shared vision and change our behavior, attitude or the words we use to get back to our plan."

Emily and Simone: Routines

"Chapter 5 with all the day-to-day examples was filled with parallels for us. No wonder our daily lives seem so stressful and tense. We are almost on the same page, but not really. Here is an example. In the past Emily would make out a schedule for everything that was going on during the week so we had a clear picture of where we needed to be, with what kid and what to bring. I thought this was great but a bit over the top, as life with kids is in a constant state of flux. But I humored her and went along with it. My idea of a routine is having a consistent, reliable . . . well maybe this will help explain: our six year old has very long curly hair. The hair routine goes like this: brush the hair thoroughly before she gets into the shower. Make sure that she gets lots of conditioner on and she leaves it in while she is washing. Towel dry the hair gently and spray with detangler. Comb the hair out completely and then braid or wrap until it dries. It's laughable. So when we got to routines, we thought we would be either on the same page or exact opposites, but it turns out it's an area we both agree is important, but in completely different ways. What we did realize immediately is that we are both way too rigid when it comes to routines. So, we started there. We redefined routines, their benefits, their downsides and how we could incorporate them into life with our kids without making life rigid and complicated. And, we realized we hadn't included the kids' ideas in any of our routines, so that answered the question of why we got so much pushback from them. After we redefined routines for our family, we sat the kids down and apologized first for being so bossy and then asked them to help us. Lo and behold, they knew exactly how we could all benefit from a few routines and at their suggestion, we tried a few for two weeks. Success. Those gray areas hold lots of opportunities for growth and change in everyone. Now when either of us starts getting too rigid, we ask the kids to give us a reality check and they quickly bring us back into balance."

Diverging

Jessica and Erin: Parenting Roles

"My father ignored my mother and all the work she put into her parenting. If she had a family meal planned, he would announce it was a good night for a picnic and a run through the nearest fast food joint would be the perfect meal. When I was young I thought this was pretty cool, but as I got older and watched as my mother's face announced her disappointment and hurt, it became much less palatable and I began to hate my father for it. I vowed that my partner and I would *always* be on the same page and never do to each other what my dad did to my mom. Well, I guess that would have been fine, had my partner had the same experience, but it was just the opposite. Her mother was a dictator, and the only time there was light and fun in the house is when her dad found the courage to challenge her mom and suggest they do something fun and spontaneous. She loved her father all the more for challenging her mother's tyrannical, rigid ways and made a vow to incorporate this into her parenting role without wondering how it might affect the relationship with her partner. As a result, there has always been an undercurrent between us, and if I suspected she would come home and squash our plans, I would dig my heels in and prepare for battle saying the kids needed consistency and routine, when in truth, that had nothing to do with why I was digging in, and if I was set on doing something the way I planned it, she would work harder to toss it for something more adventurous.

As soon as we shared our stories, we understood immediately why we were attacking each other, but we also found a small intersection (we both appreciate the balance of freedom with order) and how we could use that as our starting point and a frame of reference if we found ourselves off course. Communicating clearly, being mindful not to take things personally and taking responsibility for what is yours are key factors in our success as a co-parenting couple. In truth, we never imagined overcoming this particular obstacle, but once we did, it gave our marriage and our parenting new energy, and with it a renewed commitment to work together for the good of our family."

Kevin and Emily: Emotional Support

Kevin shared, "My dad was around, but he wasn't there. He had very little to do with me whenever I was experiencing emotional upset. He just disappeared, left it to my mom and didn't even bother to ask me about it after the fact. I vowed I would not be anything like him with my kids and would remain available if they were upset. No running away for me."

Emily explains, "My mother was a total busy-body. She wanted to know everything and she couldn't be trusted with the information she uncovered from one of our 'visits.' As a result, I made the decision that I would give my children loads of space and privacy to process their lives without interference."

Kevin continues, "The problem, as you can guess, is that I had no role model for what this looked like, and so I butted in too much, wanted to know too much, asked prying questions instead of opening space for a natural conversation and every time I did, my wife would come at the situation with guns blazing, telling me to back off and give the kid space. Neither one of us was taking into account what our child needed. We were not only ignoring each other's history, but ignoring the kid we were actually living with who, in the end, guided us toward a happy medium. We have since come up with signals to help each of us maintain some balance, boundaries and common sense when our children are experiencing a bit of emotional upheaval in their lives. Vicki shares this same statement with every parent she works with: 'Your kids are telling you everything you need to know in order to parent them successfully. The experts you are looking for to guide your parenting are living in your home; all you have to do is access them.' It's easy to disregard this as nothing more than a clever antidote used to encourage parents, but we have come to accept that she is absolutely right."

Janie and Jason: Friendship

Janie indicates, "We were a very private family, which means we didn't have a lot of friends. We didn't go to other people's homes and we didn't have friends over to our house often. I don't know why, but that is what I remember, along with feeling a deep sense of peace and connection with my family. We camped and visited museums and went to concerts and did everything together. And because we knew each other so well, we knew we would have a good time doing whatever it was we decided to do. I think I wanted to recreate that feeling of deep connection and satisfaction with my own kids and truly believed that family was enough and that kids shouldn't be pushed to make a lot of friends and to spend more time with them than they did with their own family."

Jason says, "We were a very social family, and I loved the fact that our house was the place to be if you were a kid between the ages of five and fifteen. My parents opened our homes to all of my friends. They had a few rules, and they enforced them, but by and large it was one fun day after another. It wasn't just my friends that visited; my parents had an active social life and I grew up believing that friendships were as important as family. I remember saying to my parents that when I got to be a dad, I was going to make sure that all my kids friends played at our house, and I would maintain the friendships from high school and college, which I did."

"Janie and I spent so much time trying to convince each other that 'our way' was the 'right way' that we missed what we were really trying to share with each other. This exercise gave us a neutral platform to talk about our childhoods without fear of judgment. Over time, we have found creative ways to balance out Janie's need for family time and my need for social time. Here is what we learned: our kids have their own needs and rhythms, and we weren't taking into account what they wanted. So, we asked them, and they told us. We have one very social kid, and we have a child who is so comfortable in his own skin that he just doesn't require a lot of friends. If we had known that all of our parenting decisions should be based on the kids we are raising rather than on trying to recreate or reject our own childhood memories, it would have cleared up this entire misunderstanding years ago. As it is, we have a plan, carefully crafted by both of us to allow our kids to explore the world of friendships, and we will be there to answer questions, support them and share our own experiences. We have left behind the need to convince our kids that one way is better than another."

Pam and Gwen: Sleeping

Pam and Gwen agreed that they did not want their child sleeping with them past the age of six months, when their pediatrician explained the child could sleep through the night without an additional bottle or breast. They agree that while the baby is nursing, they will keep the child in bed with them for easy nursing and maximum sleep opportunities for everyone concerned.

However, when six months arrives and Gwen is anxious to reclaim her sleeping space and her wife, Pam informs her that "the baby isn't ready."

I have heard hundreds of stories just like this one. When it comes time to follow-through on the agreement a couple has made together, parents diverge, and what was once a solid plan now becomes a point of contention. So who wins the disagreement? Is it the nursing mother? The working partner? Is it the marriage? No matter who "wins," someone "loses," and in that moment, a small, infinitesimal resentment is created. The parent whose wishes are overlooked or ignored will carry that resentment like a small stone in their breast pocket. Over time, if the sleeping issue isn't resolved in a way that makes both partners feel like it was a win, and as other areas of their co-parenting life begin to erode, the resentment begins to envelop other areas of the relationship.

Gwen and Pam went back and examined, not where things went wrong, as that was easy to pinpoint, but rather what they both believed about the situation that had them stuck.

Gwen shared the following: "I saw my parents drift apart when I was pretty young. In fact, they ended up in separate bedrooms, although they never officially ended their intimate life together. My mom was so busy with us kids, and she used that as her excuse to distance herself from my dad. She would be up late helping with homework, or watching a movie or sitting on our bed while we cried. She said she didn't want to wake my dad, but we could tell that they weren't really acting like a couple. That really scared me. Together, but not together. I didn't realize that I brought that worry into my own relationship with Pam. I was so scared of the same thing happening that I wanted the baby out quickly so we could resume our intimate relationship. I can see now that anytime I perceived her getting too involved with the kids, I would start to question the strength of our relationship and her commitment to us as a couple."

Pam had her own story, which involved a mother who was distant and made Pam feel a sense of loss and aloneness for most of her life. She remembers falling in love with Gwen and finally feeling truly connected and safe with another human being. When the baby was born, she transferred that feeling on to the child, but what really tripped her up was her belief that a child who cried and was turned away from their mother would always feel the way she did as a child.

In the case of Pam and Gwen, their trip-ups were based on their own childhood experiences and the beliefs they constructed that then became their default parenting decisions. But there was something else at play. When I talked further with Pam, it became clear that she was also afraid of what it meant to have a child who was upset. And by upset I mean any tears or in Pam's words, "a small boo-boo face leaves me feeling inadequate as a mother." In order to move forward, Pam would need Gwen's strength, encouragement and the ability to replace her faulty belief with a healthy one, which included the idea that all children will experience a wide range of emotions, and attentive and well-grounded parents will learn not to take them personally or use them as a gauge for how much they love their child or how fabulous a parent they are—even fantastic parents. Without it, both the marriage and her parenting partnership, as well as her child, were at risk.

Index

on me and 27–8; overview of 25; passive aggressive messages and 26–7; trip-ups of life and 33–40
passive aggressive communication style 26–7
peace/joy 39
peer parent pressure 35–7
power struggle 4
present day difficulties, parenting partners 11–23; childhood experiences and, influence of 18–23; collaboration with partner and 15–18; father participation and 12–15; overview of 11–12

routines exercises, parenting partner 102–6; freedom with structure 103–4; for fun 104–5; intersect, parallel, diverge 106; overcompensating, anxiety and 103; overview 102; prompt 102; self-discovery 102–5; sense of order 104; vision for the future 105

sarcasm 38
self-discovery/discovery: childhood experiences and 43–54; daily operations and 83–115; family relationships and 55–81; lifestyle and 117–48
self-discovery exercises 49–51; for bedtime/sleeping habits 98–101; for conflict 134–6; for dinners 85–8; for discipline 118–25; for education 145–7; for emotional health 128–31; family relationships, between you and your siblings 72–5; family relationships between you and your parents 59–62; friendships, family relationships and 77–80; impressions from childhood step 49–50; for independence 139–42; insights inspire change step 51; for manners 90–2; for money 111–13; parents as parenting partners, family relationships and 65–9; from past to present step 50; for routines 102–5; for technology 107–9; for toilet-training 94–6
shoulding 27
should word replacements 28
sibling relationships 70–5

skepticism 38
sleeping habits exercises, parenting partner 97–101; intersect, parallel, diverge 101; overview 97–8; prompt 98; self-discovery 98–101; vision for the future 101
strong partnership 68–9

technology exercises, parenting partner 106–10; as battle of wills 108–9; healthy balance of 108; intersect, parallel, diverge 110; as learning resource 107; overview 106; prompt 106–7; self-discovery 107–9; setting guidelines 107; social aspect of 109; as special treat 108; vision for the future 109–10
toilet-training exercises, parenting partner 93–7; intersect, parallel, diverge 97; overview 93; prompt 94; self-discovery 94–6; vision for the future 96–7
trip-ups of life *see* parenting decisions, children's responses to

vision for the future exercises 51–3; for bedtime/sleeping habits 101; for conflict 136–7; for dinners 88–9; for discipline 125–6; for education 147–8; for emotional health 131–2; family relationships, between you and your siblings 75–6; family relationships between you and your parents 62–3; friendships, family relationships and 80; for independence 143; for manners 92–3; for money 113; parents as parenting partners, family relationships and 69–70; for routines 105; for technology 109–10; for toilet-training 96–7

Walton, Frank 20, 22, 56; *see also* "The Most Memorable Observation" exercise
"Well Family" (blog) 13
working together 153–4; diverging ideas, of respect 169–71; intersecting ideas, of bedtimes 166–8; parallel ideas, of independence 168–9; parenting plan creating 158–65; partnership creating 151–8